Additional Praise

"Cyril Wong tells a simple and stylish [...] bullet and aimed at the heart of liberal [...] is also an age-old story of the child who [...] the 'good adult' whom life is not done rebuking. Do not give this book to an unsuspecting retiring teacher—unless he or she utterly deserves it."
—GWEE LI SUI, literary critic, poet, and graphic novelist

"Cyril Wong is proving himself to be a prose stylist of a calibre that threatens to outdo his poetry, with words so poignant and heartfelt, and a narrative drive that's often direct and bold yet breathtaking in its fragile beauty."
—GERRIE LIM, author of *Inside the Outsider*

"Wong pulls the rug from under us but leaves us still standing, albeit transported...to a new vantage point and offered a different perspective."
—DR K. K. SEET, prominent academic and author

"Wong writes profoundly...on what he senses as being the real challenge for most of us...to make meanings of our discontinuous worlds."
—KIRPAL SINGH, poet, cultural critic and creativity guru

"Cyril...sculpts a space for the reader to think, baffle over and be elated."
—*The Business Times*

"[A] talented writer who can write whatever he wants, with daring and originality."
—O THIAM CHIN, *The Jakarta Post*

ALSO BY THE AUTHOR

POETRY

The Dictator's Eyebrow
Straw, Sticks, Brick
Satori Blues
Oneiros
Tilting Our Plates to Catch the Light
Excess Baggage and Claim, co-authored with Terry Jaensch
Like a Seed with Its Singular Purpose
Unmarked Treasure
Below: Absence
The End of His Orbit
Squatting Quietly

PROSE

Let Me Tell You Something About That Night

THE LAST LESSON
of
MRS DE SOUZA

A NOVEL

CYRIL WONG

EPIGRAM BOOKS / SINGAPORE

Copyright © 2013 by Cyril Wong

All rights reserved
Published in Singapore by Epigram Books
www.epigrambooks.sg

Edited by Jason Erik Lundberg
Cover design by Lydia Wong
Layout by Maliah Zubir

Published with the support of

NATIONAL ARTS COUNCIL
SINGAPORE

National Library Board, Singapore
Cataloguing-in-Publication Data

Wong, Cyril, 1977-
The last lesson of Mrs de Souza : a novel / Cyril Wong. – Singapore :
Epigram Books, 2013.
p. cm

ISBN: 978-981-07-6232-2 (paperback)
ISBN: 978-981-07-6233-9 (ebook)

1. Teachers – Fiction. 2. Teacher-student relationships – Fiction. I. Title.

PR9570.S53 W57
S823 -- dc23   OCN855190257

This is a work of fiction. Names, characters, places, and incidents either are the product of the author's imagination or are used fictitiously. Any resemblance to actual persons, living or dead, events, or locales is entirely coincidental.

First Edition: October 2013
10 9 8 7 6 5 4 3 2 1

For the teachers who made all the difference,
especially Roslyn Seah and the late Rita Leicester.

CHAPTER 1

I AM SIXTY years old this morning. I have decided that enough is enough.

Today is to be my last day of teaching. The 1990s will be here next year, signifying a promising start, a new phase in my life. I might be old but my health is good; unlike my poor late husband, I could live up to a hundred. I want to travel again. I even plan to write creatively, or paint, or learn to play more difficult pieces of classical music on the piano; maybe something by Gershwin or Debussy. Maybe I just want to do as little as possible in my retirement years. I am really not quite sure what I will do once I have left school for good. As I fantasise about my future, I am also preparing to go to work, drinking my daily glass of orange juice in the kitchen and picking up my files one last time from the dining table, before breezing out from my spacious three-room flat to take the lift to the ground floor, then walking to where my maroon-coloured Mazda is waiting in the public parking lot outside. I do not even bother to catch a glimpse of myself in the car's rear-view mirror, as I already know that my lipstick is impeccably applied; my hair is also, as usual, perfectly in place.

After placing the files on the seat next to mine, I realise that I have forgotten to do my usual meditation practice this morning. I always meditate for half an hour after I wake up and before I take a shower. But it is also my birthday today, which could be why I have forgotten. Not that today being my birthday is any big deal. I stopped caring about birthdays decades ago. Yet there is still a part of me that nonetheless anticipates the array of birthday cards and flowers (my students usually cannot afford anything more) that will miraculously appear on my table when I step into the classroom later. Such gifts are more often than not a result of custom and formality, something that students in the school have always done because they have felt obliged to do so when it came to 'special' occasions like a birthday or Teachers' Day. At the same time, I am convinced that at least a few of the gifts will be sincerely given. I have never expected everyone to like me in the classroom; but I also know that, as a teacher, I have not been particularly unkind or unreasonable either; in fact, I believe that I have been sufficiently warm-hearted and generous towards my boys for the time that I have instructed them. I am certain that some of them are genuinely gratified by this, and will express their gratitude and respect through their gifts.

But first things first. I rest both my hands on the steering wheel and close my eyes.

Meditation is important to me. I am not Buddhist—in fact, I am not particularly religious in any sense—but I am a firm believer in the healthy effects of meditation, and a general believer in the intrinsic goodness of all life. I have neither believed that the driving force of creation possesses a personality that can be summed up by any holy book, nor that existence is a gaping void that eats at the soul, as Existentialist philosophers would have it. I mostly believe, deep in my bones, that life is very simply beyond description; regardless of what one makes of it, life always spills over the parameters of how anyone has chosen to define it.

As my eyes stay closed, with the breath moving slowly in and out of my lungs, I think about my late husband. It was Christopher de Souza who taught me about how meditation is a practice that is universal, transcending any talk of faith or religious denominations. From Hindu sadhus in India to Tibetan monks to French Christian mystics, meditation is a common practice that helps a person return to a state of untainted awareness, as well as an awareness of one's surroundings, and all without preconceived notions, judgements, the ups and downs of turbulent emotions, or even pain. It was meditation that helped Christopher when his body fought against pancreatic cancer in the last weeks of his life.

"Rose," Christopher said one time at the hospital when I visited him, not knowing that we were nearing the last few days of our time together, "do you know that when I meditate, the pain seems to move further and further away? It is as if you become part of something larger than yourself, so that pain becomes only a small part of all that you can be."

I remember stroking his back as he described this. This memory is followed by a flashback-summary (for some unknowable reason, such flashbacks occur more frequently in my life now that I am older) of all the events leading up to his eventual death, from the quarrels we had (started mostly by me) whenever I tried to dissuade him from mentioning his death (a fact I did not need reminding of), to his sudden bloating after meals, the escalating weight loss (I had never seen him look so sallow and gaunt in our thirty years of marriage), and then the jaundiced hue of his skin that became disturbingly pronounced during the week before he passed away. He died in his sleep in his hospital bed. His death happened while I was asleep on the visitor's couch that had been moved so I could sit closer to my husband. I had already been so exhausted from staying up late every night before the very evening he gave up on his life and left me for good.

I really had wanted to be awake when it happened, or to be there, at the very least, to hold his hand while he gasped one last time, or whatever the living are supposed to do, voluntarily or otherwise, at the moment of the spirit's departure. I had also wanted to say "I'll miss you" or, even better, "I love you". I had hoped that he would find the last-minute strength to say some final words to me too, something moving and memorable.

Thankfully, as it is still early in the morning, no neighbours are walking past my car while I am inside, wondering if there is something odd about the old but elegant Eurasian woman clutching the steering wheel with her eyes firmly closed. Finally, I open my eyes and gaze out onto the car park that brightens with every new breath I take. I miss Christopher, but he is gone. I insert my car key, turn on the engine, and begin my slow and careful drive to school.

CHAPTER 2

TODAY HAPPENS TO be the last day before the school holidays. Class 3S2 (supposedly the second-best class at that level, based on the students' marks from the previous year) is waiting for their teacher to 'float' into the classroom. Another teacher told me once that he overheard one of my students, Subra (the rude one), joking in the canteen to another classmate, Zhang Wei, about how their English teacher looks like an alien-lollipop whenever anyone spots her from across a distance. According to Subra (who is not the first student to have described me like this, or said something similar), the effect of my appearance is heightened by the way I seem almost to hover a few centimetres off the ground whenever I walk. This must be because I am a tall, skinny woman (not slender and not even slightly curvaceous), with hair like a coiffed cloud rising up above my shoulders; if my permed hair got any bigger, according to someone like Subra, it might carry me off into the sky like a hot air balloon.

To be honest, I cannot remember when it was exactly that I decided on my present hairstyle. I suppose it was partly the way my hair naturally grew, which could get quite unruly (like my late mother's hair, a messy head of wild curls); and a regular day every month at the salon has ensured that my hair stays in place, resulting in its eventual state and unchanging shape over time. Maybe the way I have kept my hair in check has something to do with not wanting to look like my mother, whose messy hair somehow reflected or emphasised her disgruntled and erratic personality. I blame the way I walk or 'float' on my days growing up in a convent girls' school, where teachers were always berating us young ladies for our bad postures whenever we sat with a slouch, or shuffled from one classroom to another. These were the teachers I admired; loomingly composed figures who were stern, even slightly frosty, but who never lost their temper at anyone; whose heads were held up and whose noses hovered haughtily over the heads of students; impressive figures (especially the female teachers) who seemed warm when required to appear generous and approachable, but who never lost their overall cool in the way that they addressed a room full of impressionable, adolescent girls. I remember admiring such teachers, looking up to them, wanting to behave, talk and look like them; it was likely they made me want to become a teacher, so I could one day transform *into* them. Perhaps the fact that these teachers were so different from my graceless and temperamental mother was why I hoped to emulate them so much; to be poised, semi-aristocratic and flawlessly groomed.

In time, my globular hairdo became iconic at St Nicholas Boys' School. Colleagues and students throughout the years have tended to marvel (sometimes openly or presumably amongst themselves) at how my hair has always managed to keep its roundish, gravity-defying shape. I am also apparently known for wearing either dark green or red dresses to school

("Mrs Christmas de Souza," another student once joked, when he thought I had long left the classroom), the colours standing out in contrast to my dark, smooth skin. Sticking to such colours for my wardrobe is mostly a matter of convenience; it can be exhausting to dress differently for work every day. This is not to say that vanity has not played its part in my choice of clothes. I might be sixty, but I can still pass as forty-something because of the glimmering darkness of my pigmentation and the clothes I choose to wear; although if you look closely enough, wrinkles are already starting to cluster around my eyes.

More importantly, I hope that even after I have left this institution for good, my present students will have some fond memories of my strict but approachable teaching style, my occasional kindness and warmth; that they will not resent me if ever I seemed cold or even sarcastic (something over which I have had little control in my later years) whenever someone made a poorly considered remark or offered an incorrect answer in class. Today, as all my students stand up for the last time to greet me good morning, I notice (just as I anticipated) that the table at the front of the room is covered in cards wishing me Happy Birthday or bearing poignant messages of farewell. There are even bunches of different flowers wrapped in foil or brown paper. I only have an hour with my classroom of boys today; afterwards they will leave for other classes to convey their farewells to other teachers who have taught them for this academic year.

"Good morning, class. Please, sit down," I say in a clear voice. I step, or 'float', to the front of the class and try to find a place on my overcrowded table to put down my files. All the boys say "Thank you" in unison, their voices suddenly filling me with a sense of nostalgia that I have never experienced before. Then they sit back down, noisily dragging the legs of their chairs against the dusty classroom floor. Instead of standing beside my table with my arms behind my back, as I usually do whenever I am preparing to address the class, I decide that I too will sit down at my table today. The boys are visibly puzzled. They watch as the teacher who has taught them to write better essays and express themselves through creative writing compositions now sits in silence for a whole minute with arms folded, my gaze temporarily lost amidst the cards and the flowers piled up haphazardly before me. The boys are not sure if I am merely taking a moment to contain my happiness or surprise. Zhang Wei, one of the most outspoken boys in class, the one I have often picked to answer questions when nobody else would put up their hands, breaks the silence and asks in a tentative voice from across the room: "You okay, Mrs de Souza?"

They all must know that today is also their teacher's last day of school before retirement. Perhaps, in their minds, I appear slightly despondent, and need a moment to keep my emotions in check. When I first walked into the classroom, I was, at first, extremely pleased by the gifts I saw on my table. My first thought was a happy one: it is wonderful to be appreciated, even though I am already used to being appreciated, sincerely or otherwise, by my students over the years. I have been a teacher longer than any other teacher in this institution. I have seen countless boys (from mischievous students to lazy and deceitful ones to obedient and respectful ones) come and go, colleagues enter their careers fresh and bumbling and then leave as poor jaded souls, the walls of the classrooms fade from deep yellow to pastel (*Such a hideous colour*, I thought to myself when renovations were completed); I have also watched my husband shrivel away to nothing.

This is my last day of teaching. For so long, I have not known how to be anything else. The thought of this, without warning, weighs heavily on my mind. So heavy, in fact, that I have to sit down and fold my arms. Distantly, I *am* still glad to see the expressions of appreciation stacked up on my desk. I know that I will look back on this moment with some nostalgia and over-sentimentality, regardless of how perfunctory such gestures of appreciation have often been. The past can appear more idyllic and less truthful through the eyes of the future. Some effort, nonetheless, went into writing these cards. Amidst the gifts, there has to be at least one that originated from the heart. Soon a deluge of memories passes through me in the span of a minute. After which, an open and vacant future appears somewhere at the front of my brain; a single thought that expands and threatens to draw me away completely from the present moment...before I realise that forty pairs of eyes are observing me curiously from beyond my table.

I wonder what the boys must think as I brush aside any distracting remnant of thought from my mind. I try to smile. I start to look more intently at my students now from where I am sitting. This is the last class of students I will ever teach in my life. "Sorry about that, boys," I say at last, and look over at Zhang Wei with some semblance of affection. "Thank you, Zhang Wei. I'm fine."

I gaze across at all of my boys and begin to speak at length: "I was just thinking...since it is to be our last day together in school, and yes, I'm feeling a little sad that I'll have to see you all go, I thought that maybe we can do something different for a change. Maybe we can have a chat, and then I promise we will finish promptly on the hour, so you may arrive punctually for your next class. Your other teachers must have arranged some special activities for you. How about it then? How about for this short time that you have left with me, we just have a chat?"

Some boys turn to eyeball each other with varying degrees of puzzlement. Most continue to stare at me with uncertainty as I sit behind my table, wondering if I am truly fine. A few boys nod at my suggestion. My behaviour must appear indeed strange today. Usually I would be standing or pacing up and down the classroom, giving instructions or talking. Some students in the past have asked about why my voice bears traces of a British accent; I answered that I did not quite know, or that I probably developed the accent back in my own school days when those teachers who instructed me would have originally studied in England. Some students have even dared to ask about my manicured nails, which I would hide by placing my hands behind my back as I talked; I would put them behind my back even more self-consciously as time went by, so as not to invite closer inspection and unnecessary commentary. I have never responded well to such questions regarding my appearance from my boys and have tended to avoid such topics altogether by throwing questions back at them about their schoolwork. I suppose that this is because I am still a little shy about the way I look; especially with members of the opposite sex, regardless of their age. My insecurities, as regards my vanity, betray me during such moments. A woman's appearance is always important to her, regardless of whether she is married or not; or especially after she has turned single again after her husband's demise. With arms folded gently across my chest now, I become aware of my dark red nails digging slightly into my skin. I must be feeling tense.

As the years passed, more students also began to ask me about my ethnicity or cultural background. "'Eurasian'? What does 'Eurasian' mean, Mrs de Souza?" Even though St Nicholas is officially a missionary school, it accepts boys of various religious backgrounds; from Muslims, Hindus and Taoists to students with no religious upbringing at all. The reason for this has surely been economic, given that Catholics have never made up a huge section of the country's population. During the occasional morning mass in the school's chapel organised for particularly important days in the Roman Catholic calendar, such as Ash Wednesday or the day of the Virgin Mary's Assumption, non-Catholics would hide out in their respective classrooms and wait for their friends to come back so classes could resume. St Nicholas has always been unique in bringing together boys not just of different religious backgrounds but also of different ethnicities, so even though everyone tends to speak English in school, the boys are accustomed to encountering a wide range of racial and cultural differences on a daily basis. Such differences were so commonplace that nobody thought to ask about them in any intrusive or curious way.

In time, however, I soon noticed that the students were becoming less racially diverse, with more Chinese boys forming the majority (a reflection, perhaps, of changes in the larger, expanding society). With less and less exposure to a greater mix of ethnicities in general on the school compound, more and more boys (even the non-Chinese ones) began to ask about my own background with surprising curiosity. I found that I enjoyed answering such questions, explaining such words like 'Luso-Indian' with some pride regarding my Eurasian heritage. It felt good on such occasions to be talking about more than just English vocabulary and grammar. I enjoyed feeling different or unique in this school environment. I liked being a custodian of an aspect of the country's cultural history for my students, especially with less and less Eurasians working or studying in the school as time went by. However, in later years, I grew bored of talking about my Indian-Portuguese ancestry, how Eurasians first came into being when the Dutch and the British colonised this part of the world (followed by increasing intermarriages between Europeans and Asians), and Devil's Curry (a supposedly traditional Eurasian curry dish made from Christmas leftovers; I know this only in theory, as I have almost never cooked at home). I started to sound less like a glib tourism-advert when I eventually insisted that race is more like a figment of people's collective imagination, a social construction, an illusion.

As I am reminiscing about all this now, I remember that

in the eyes of the boys before me, I am still just sitting here, silence forming a widening gulf between us. Suddenly aware that my arms are still folded, making my posture come across as a tad defensive, I unfold my arms and rest them on the table in front of me instead, nudging a few colourful birthday cards out of the way. I lean forward, symbolically closing off any distance that might have formed between my boys and me. Smiling, I speak again: "And by the way, thank you for your lovely gifts. I'm overwhelmed and I'm also very grateful. Teachers do still live for this kind of thing, you know; even though we might be old and grey."

A few boys snicker. Most of them look up automatically at my bouffant hair, a work of art or force of nature in itself, immovable and incapable of collapse. At the same time, I am aware that a few streaks of grey have appeared at the front and sides of my spherical coiffure; more and more grey strands straying and sticking out more obviously around my ears, unwilling to stay within the rigid confines of the rest of my hairdo. Despite signs of grey and the deepening wrinkles on my face, I am still confident that I have managed to look vibrant and younger than my sixty years of age. My green dress, with its textured pattern of a single flower's outline repeated as a discreet motif all over the fabric, hopefully helps to provide me with an air of cheeriness that, for a moment, diminished when I sat in silence, withdrawing into my thoughts.

"Well, you don't look that old, Teacher," Subra, another student, offers as a half-joking and wryly ironic response. A Tamil-speaking Indian boy with a polished and dark complexion and an almost-permanent sneer on his face,

Subra has mostly been a B-student with a propensity for openly making rude comments in class, mostly directed to the other boys, but sometimes also at me when he is unwilling to answer questions that I have posed. I have found that the best way to deal with boys like Subra is to be blithely ignorant of his intentions to offend, and to just keep directing the same question at him repeatedly, as if he were somewhat deaf, until he has no choice but to answer me appropriately.

"Suck-up," another boy mutters in response. It sounds like Eric Tan, the plumpest boy in the room, who usually scores the highest marks for class tests. Mostly polite, Eric has moments when he feels as if he has to fit in by imitating the mocking behaviour of his classmates. But I cannot be sure that he is the one who has spoken. The whole class is laughing now.

"Boys, why would Subra need to suck up to me?" I respond. "After all, it's my last day, right? You won't be seeing any more of me after today. Next year, a new English teacher will be taking over. Who knows, maybe you might even like her better than me."

The class falls silent at this point, some boys still wanting to joke facetiously about how they would still miss me anyway, maybe even half-meaning what they are planning to say. Eventually nobody bothers to reply. I doubt that any of them would miss me. Perhaps I have been nothing but a talking head to these boys, a walking caricature of an antiquated schoolteacher with no insight into their lives to offer beyond the refinement of their linguistic skills.

"I'm just glad that all of you will be moving on to the

next level. Secondary Four will be a tough year for all of you, you can be guaranteed of that." The concern in my voice rings slightly false in my ears. I try harder to sound more sincere and to mean what I am saying. "But that is not what I want to talk about now. Please forgive me, as it is not as if I planned in advance what I want to say. I'm still organising my thoughts even as I'm speaking to you now."

The boys are quiet, listening attentively.

"You see, I brought my work-files here, thinking that I would use my notes today to try and teach you something in preparation for next year. But I've changed my mind at the last minute. I don't really have anything to teach you that you won't probably forget over the holidays anyway. In any case, you will learn about those things in the new year, when the new teacher takes over from me. I've decided that I want to use this opportunity, this last chance, to say things that I wish I had said, or said more directly, before now."

Some of the students look at each other, curious about where this monologue is going. I can almost hear Subra's brain working at the back of the room; he must be concocting some kind of barbed response.

"So I hope you won't mind if I talk first about myself, and then you may ask me any question you like afterwards. Is that fine with all of you?"

Some boys nod carefully in agreement. Some utter aloud, but not too loudly or enthusiastically, in unison: "Yes, Teacher..."

I close my hands over one another on the table before me, speaking just a little more energetically than before. "Let's see then. You know me mostly as a teacher of the English language, somebody who has put up with more than my fair share of mischievousness from some of you. But I'm sure you can tell that I've also always encouraged you to speak your mind because I think, especially in school, that it's very important to learn to do so early on in your life. You don't want to end up like so many people in this country, or like so many of my colleagues, the other teachers who teach you, for example, the ones who behave like they've lost their souls and their will to live, the ones who appear to have given up on their inner voices. You don't want to end up becoming a zombie like so many of such people."

The boys know better than to gasp in surprise. They are too cool for that. But they are nonetheless surprised. They have very likely never heard any teacher put down other members of the teaching staff before. At the same time, most of them would likely think that if some other teacher (someone younger, for instance) were to go down this road about 'speaking your mind' and 'being true to yourself', they would guess straight away that she or he was merely trying to impress them by that contrived endeavour to appear radical, rebellious or confrontational (much like Robin Williams with his clichéd *carpe diem* proclamation from that hopelessly idealistic movie, *Dead Poets Society*, which was released earlier this year).

In this case, I suspect the boys are simply surprised that *I* am the one (the one who has always been so polite and conservative and by-the-book) who is conveying such a message. Coming from an older teacher like me, however, I am hoping that what I am saying might sound new again, even slightly controversial. In any case, even if I look stupid now in front of these mostly polite but quietly apathetic boys, what do I have to lose?

For a brief instant and without warning, the image of my late husband jumps into view. Christopher sitting at the back of my classroom now, seated somewhere beside Subra. My husband is shaking his gleaming, bald head while listening to me address my seemingly attentive students. There are wisps of grey in his eyebrows and a faint moustache is visible above his lips. He is smiling half-proudly, half-chidingly. When he was alive, Christopher was a mathematics teacher at a neighbouring school, where he was known as a strict disciplinarian. He slouched slightly when he walked, which I had feared would make him an easy target of ridicule in school; he claimed that, in fact, his slouch made him seem even more ominous to his students. Of course, I had only ever heard Christopher's account of life in his school, yet I am still certain that he was sterner than me and a more conservative teacher who would never approve of classes being used for rambling soliloquies like the one I am embarking on now (and without fully understanding why). Words just seem to stream forth from my throat at this moment. Any logical reason or explanation for this will only come to me at the end of today, when I am back at home alone after my final day of school; when I have to decide what I am going to have for my solitary dinner as another evening without Christopher dims quickly into night.

"I know some of you might think that what I'm saying is nothing new. You've probably heard it from some other teacher, from books or on television. But in this country... this society...and I cannot stress this enough, you *will* forget to remember who you are. You'll become so carried away with your own lives, with earning more and more money, with buying expensive properties you can hardly afford, with the never-ending needs of your families, until you have lost, well, everything that has made you who you are, or who you used to be. You'll think that what you are is already special because you have a job, a family, a special status in society and a beautiful home, because you lead a life undisturbed by social unrest, by any serious financial difficulty. But I'm telling you...no, I'm *warning* you: it will *not* be enough."

I pause to take a breath. The words are coming faster and faster. Gratefully, I realise that my students seem to be listening; most of them are pretending to anyway, with nobody whispering amongst themselves. (I imagine them thinking: Our teacher's old age has finally caught up with her. Maybe it's Alzheimer's or something.) I ponder about how it must be odd for them to watch me and listen to me speak like this, while on my desk, their cards remain unread, the flowers untouched. I notice a bunch of roses that seems too artificial; I am tempted to reach out and touch the plastic-looking petals, but resist the urge. The boys must have simply bought the cards and flowers from the grocery located just across the road from the back entrance of the school. It would be a convenient thing to do, requiring no great effort at all, to pick up a card or a flower, scribble something seemingly heartfelt inside a card and plonk the presents on my table. A split-second daydream flashes across my mind about how, as I am talking, my persistent voice is parting the cards and the flowers like the sea, until some of them might wash over the edges of the table and crash dramatically to the floor. It is possible that all of these boys are now just being silent and patient with me this once because it is my last class with them. They will never have to listen to Rose de Souza ever again.

It is Eric, the plump, bespectacled Chinese boy, who unexpectedly raises his hand at this point. I gesture at him to speak, glad that somebody is willing to ask a question in response to what I have said. Frowning a little, since he is probably worried that his question might irritate me, Eric asks anyway: "But Teacher, what if it *is* enough? My parents are happy, I think. They *look* like they are happy. My parents are not rich. They worked hard to put my sister and me through school. I know they think that all their hard work paid off in the end because their children are both doing well in school. So they must be happy, right? Isn't it enough for them to think like this?"

I decide to proceed carefully. "Yes, Eric. It *is* enough if they believe it is enough. If *you* really believe it is enough. But remember, Eric, parents don't tell their children everything. Parents make sacrifices so that their children will lead lives they themselves could not lead. Maybe it *is* enough for them to see their children succeed. But does that mean that parents don't also wish more for themselves too? When I was growing up, my mother—" the image of my querulous mother with her oily cheeks, wild hair and narrowed eyes comes to mind— "would constantly remind me about how unhappy she was, and how much she had to give up in terms of furthering her own studies so that *I* could have the chance to receive a proper education. A few times she would tell me she was satisfied that I had at least been a good daughter to her, but I knew that if given a second chance, and without her daughter in the picture, she would have wanted something entirely different for herself. But this is not quite what I'm trying to say about this matter of being enough."

The flushed round face of my dark-skinned mother looms large in my thoughts now. A small but loud and argumentative housewife, she had lived through a war, and given birth to me long before this country became independent. Both mother and father worked hard to make ends meet so that their daughter could lead a comfortable existence. Although I remember my father to be a kindly man, a businessman who was always away on trips abroad, his marriage to my mother was a troubled one. My mother used to tell me that there were times when she hated being stuck at home, taking care of meals and countless household chores, on top of the ever-fickle whims and fancies of her only daughter. Mother longed to travel, to study philosophy and music, to taste foreign foods, meet new people. She had never been satisfied just being the not-too-passive, frumpy, Indian housewife married to her tall, skinny, fair-skinned, Luso-Indian husband who travelled all the time, making important deals and shaking hands with American and European businessmen overseas.

Having a hunch (such instincts sharpened by my years of teaching) that Eric might really have more to say about his family, I now ask him pointedly: "Do you feel that your parents are perfectly satisfied with their lives? As children, all of us have special ways of knowing whether our parents are truly happy or not. We know it without really knowing it, even without trying to find out."

"I still think they are happy, most of the time...but sometimes, I think, maybe I can tell when my father isn't completely happy when he's stuck at home with the rest of us."

"How do you mean, Eric?"

"There are times..." Eric hesitates. He looks like he is remembering something he has not been prepared to remember, especially not today of all days, with the holidays just around the corner and the fun things he has been hoping to do with family and friends during a much needed break from school. Perhaps I'm having an unexpected effect on my students, maybe even a dramatic and positive one. "There are times when I see my father watching television. He watches television more and more now. And I know he watches it because he doesn't really want to be at home; he'd rather be out there with his friends or travelling somewhere. He always flares up when I try to ask him anything while he's watching his favourite shows. Maybe it also has something to do with my mother. Maybe he's trying not to think about my mother. Mum usually comes back home late from work now. I don't know why. I'm not sure she's really working late. Actually, I don't know anything at all. Like you said, I just have a feeling about both of them."

Everyone in the classroom listens very carefully. Eric is quite possibly the smartest student in class. He is also usually quite reserved (as reserved as any student would be who is ashamed to stand out in a classroom for his eagerness to learn, and who appears to know the answers to any question posed by the teacher) but he always scores A's for class tests and exams. I am guessing that most of them must have never heard Eric speak like this before. Everyone is surprised, including me. I wonder if perhaps a few students might have some inkling about Eric's family life, as some must have visited Eric at his home where they would study together before crucial tests. They might have even been introduced to Eric's parents, so some of the things Eric is saying now could be resonating with them. Eric could have also dropped a few hints during conversations about what he felt about his family, whenever his friends stayed over. I scan the classroom briefly. Some of Eric's friends, one or two boys with a possibly deeper familiarity regarding Eric's family situation, now turn away to look elsewhere, possibly embarrassed for him; although from their faces, I can still tell that they are also interested in what else Eric has to say.

I stare at Eric and nod, urging him to carry on. Eric glimpses down at his table, as if contemplating for a second whether to pick up a pen and play with it while he continues to speak. In the end, he leaves the pen alone and addresses the rest of the class and me: "It's really just a feeling. I have no proof or anything. When my sister and I are around, they seem really okay together. All of us even went to Johor last Christmas. I thought we had a good time. But the rest of the time, I just think…I get the sense that they're really avoiding each other. My father loves to watch documentaries and I've seen how my mother looks at him when he's on the sofa watching his programmes. She always looks angry when she's watching him, like he's doing something wrong. And I see how she sometimes looks at the house phone too when she thinks nobody is looking; when my father's not noticing her. She is always waiting for some friend to call her at home; someone who would make her smile when the call comes. Maybe it's her friends asking her to go out with them or something, but she can't go out because she has to be home with us, with her family. I know she doesn't want to be home if she can help it. I can see it in her eyes. It's as though she wants to get away from us and go out, but she can't because we're all there, expecting her to stay home."

This is turning out to be a long one-on-one between Eric and me, with the rest of the class watching and none of them offering any meaningful input. I think for a moment and respond: "Look, Eric, it's not my place to say anything bad about your family. But you yourself know best about what's happening with your situation at home. Maybe you're right. Maybe at the end of the day, your parents might believe that there's ultimately nothing wrong with their lives. No one can really say that they know exactly what another person is thinking or feeling, especially when the other person doesn't make the time to talk to you, even if the person is your mother or father."

Then I address the rest of the class: "Only *you* can know what you yourself are feeling at any moment in your life. Only *you* can fix the problems in your own life. I'm sure you can agree with me on this."

All eyes are trained on their English teacher. I must act and sound like somebody they are meeting for the first time.

Only Eric has turned his head to gaze out the window, thinking about the things that he unwittingly told his classmates, unsure of what they might think of him after today. He might be hoping the holidays will help them forget that he has even spoken up in class.

The image of Christopher now gets up from where he has supposedly been sitting at the back of the class. My bald and now slightly haggard husband slowly walks out of the room, but not before pausing to look at me one last time, smiling cryptically. Why am I imagining this at all? Am I secretly worried that the class is getting bored? Is my private sense of worry manifesting as the still handsome but increasingly emaciated face of my late husband leaving me now for yet another time? But Christopher is also smiling—tenderly, maybe even encouragingly. This is my waking dream, my self-created fantasy about my husband, after all; I can make him feel anything I want him to feel, or look like how I want him to look, just as he is now drifting out of my classroom and out of my imagination. I am certain that if Christopher was here for real, he would, in fact, be egging me on. He used to assure me that I *am* making a difference in my students' lives; that I *am* a good teacher, even when I might not always believe it. At this moment, at least, I am starting to feel that perhaps he was right. I have done my best, after all. Like now, with Eric piping up about his family, these are the moments that illustrate that I am making a positive difference by encouraging my students to be more thoughtful, more self-aware, more outspoken; I am making my students better and stronger people, even if they might not even know it.

Then another image invades my mind, one that is crueller because it is based on something that actually happened. It is from a moment during the last few days before he died. "I hope I've made you happy," Christopher said to me, my hand in his. This was right after a painful argument (painful because my husband looked too weak to argue with me; I felt as if I was draining him by forcing my point of view upon him) about whether to keep him on life support if he lost consciousness completely (Christopher said "no", whereas my stance was an emotional "yes"). He looked so pale and jaundiced laying in the hospital bed, a sharp contrast to the bright blue of his hospital gown, his hand trembling slightly over mine.

I repress a grievous sigh, and carry on talking to my class. "You have to try and remind yourself, all the time, about whether you have done all you can to lead a meaningful life; whether you have done all you can to be honest with yourself and to be happy; so that you will not be filled with regret when you're old and dying. Do you understand what I'm trying to say?"

Everyone is peering closely at me, not sure whether to nod or just to stare blankly. For an instant, I am unsure if anything I have said is sinking in. The fact remains that I have, at the very least, tried my best to warn my students about their possible futures and what can happen if they are not careful. It is my last day of school! I can do nothing else but try, especially today! If only I had been less passive in my attempts in the past to improve the way my students thought about their lives; the most I have ever done has been to encourage students to voice their true and honest opinions in creative writing compositions, to speak bravely and intelligently during lessons, or offer unique perspectives on newspaper articles that I would hand out for their critical perusal. I should have been more direct with my boys!

Subra raises his hand to ask a question. I brace myself for what he might say, which will likely be designed to offend. I nod at him, noticing the wide expense of his forehead receding into hair that has been neatly combed and gelled back. "Mrs de Souza, how about you? Can you say that you're happy then? I mean, you've been a teacher for so long. Have you done all *you* can to be true to who you are, and to lead a happy, meaningful life?"

In a half-conscious way, I know that I have been expecting this question. I am also not terribly surprised that the question has come from Subra. I gaze at the fan spinning on the ceiling, gathering my thoughts. "No, Subra. I think you can say that I'm not happy; or at least, I'm not as happy as I set out to be."

Nobody says a word for a while. Subra's newly puzzled expression makes him seem as if he is thinking about something imponderable. It is Zhang Wei who then breaks the silence, without raising his hand, with that inevitable question: "Why?"

I turn my head at this point to gaze out the window at the empty school field outside, the very spaciousness that I would lose myself in when I felt my mind stuttering with too many questions from students for whom I had no answers. I will miss that view of the field after today, the relief that it has given me during my most stressful moments in class. I turn back, glancing quickly at the faces of all the boys in the room. "Well, first and most of all, I miss my husband, Mr Christopher de Souza."

I wonder whether my husband will appear now if I look back at the school field gleaming in the sun outside, waiting to greet my tired eyes with a smile and a wave. Would he be walking along the running track that surrounds the field, or standing perhaps by the goalpost, grinning with his shiny head cocked to one side?

"My husband died a few years ago from cancer. It seems that everyone dies from cancer these days, right? Nobody just dies any more, with the heart collapsing from weariness, the brain just stopping to fire up in the morning when you wake. It was a painful death for Mr de Souza; he went through the whole agonising process of chemotherapy, of dying, like a hero...my hero."

I pause. I am afraid to turn my head in the direction of the window again; although the temptation is great, especially now.

At first, the class is almost too still. The silence is like a dinosaur in the centre of the room, which everyone pretends is not really there. Then heads swivel slowly away or drop heavily down. Nobody asks any questions. Nobody wants to disturb the silence, for fear that it might start to move, pushing against chairs and tables, or grow and swell into something worse, something limitless and uncontainable.

I carry on. "Missing my husband is only part of it. It's a huge part, but it's only a part. Maybe I'm being unduly pessimistic. Maybe I should try to regain some perspective. I think, regarding most of my life, I could say that I've been happy, although I wouldn't say that I've been completely satisfied. I loved my husband, and my husband loved me very much. This is not to say we didn't fight; we quarrelled about many things, such as what it means to be a good teacher. We did our best, individually and as a couple; we each tried to make a difference in the world. He's a part of me now, even though he has left me for good. I know this to be true, even if people can argue that I'm simply lying to myself. It doesn't matter. I believe this to be true. It's good enough, because it has to be."

Some of the students are nodding, almost unconsciously. They must have half-expected me to burst into tears. I am managing not to cry. Maybe there are no more tears left within me. Then comes a condescending thought: here are students seeming to commiserate with me on my personal loss, boys who have only just left the awkward phases of puberty a handful of years behind them. What do they know about death, or about moving on from death? Then I am reminded of my meditational practice this morning in my car. I become conscious of my breath moving in and out of me now, the way Christopher once taught me to deal with pain.

Yet who am I to judge the young? Have all my years of teaching and dealing with boys taught me nothing about their own unique wealth of experiences? Who is to say that my students have not also endured the death of a relative or a friend? Yet it cannot possibly be the same thing. Losing the love of your life has to be the worst thing in the world. How many of these boys will meet the love of their lives, let alone learn how to outlive their beloved partner in life?

"Maybe I'm wrong. Maybe losing the love of your life is not the worst thing in the world," I say, thinking aloud. "There could be worse things, such as not having known love at all. But this isn't what I'm talking about. What I was saying is this." I know I am scrambling for a moment, to get back on track. "I wish, in all my years as a teacher, that I had been smarter. I wish I had been braver and more attentive. It's not as if I never stood up for what I believed in, but I think I could have done more. There was this one time…"

It must be the fact that this is my last day in school that the memories are flooding back, such as memories or fantasies about Christopher, unbuckled emotions rising up from a once-dormant part of my mind. After another moment's pause, as I lean back more comfortably into my chair with hands folded gently on my lap, I realise, at last, which story from my past I have been meaning (and not quite consciously wanting) to tell.

CHAPTER 3

FOR A MOMENT, there is nobody in the classroom except for me, and Amir. He is sitting at his usual desk. My memory must be failing me, since I cannot see his face clearly; it is blurry, even though he is not sitting very far from where I am standing. My chest tightens a little and I am not sure why. Amir is raising his hand to catch my attention, even though I am obviously the only other person in the room. I think he wants to ask a question regarding something I have said, a lesson that I have been giving. Amir has always been eager to learn. I sense that his mouth is moving, but no words can be heard. His face remains a wilful blur. I want to say something in response, even though I have not heard his question, even though all of this is merely happening inside my imagination. For some reason, I have an irrational hope that if I give the correct answer right now inside this daydream, I might fix the past completely.

It must have been about fifteen years ago when it happened. I cannot remember it 'like it was yesterday', as the saying goes. Even now, as I am relating this story about Amir, I cannot confidently recall his facial features with forensic exactness. I cannot even remember if he had a crew cut or a slight fringe for a hairstyle.

I do remember that his hair was neat and somewhat short; that he was not particularly tall, fat or unhealthily thin; that his darkish skin was slightly pockmarked from acne; that he did not like taking part in soccer games which the boys played not just during Physical Education lessons, but after school as well. I do know that he had a shy but pleasant, almost attractive, smile; slightly crooked, which added to Amir's appeal. In the classroom now, I refrain from mentioning any of these descriptive details, for fear that I might be straying too far from the truth. And the truth, or my version of what I consider the truth, is important to me, especially in relating this story today.

However, as I tell my story, I choose not to mention Amir's name. I will also not mention much of what he told me in confidence. I know that if I reveal too much, the boys might fixate childishly on all the wrong elements of Amir's story, instead of the intrinsic truth that I want to convey, which is that I made a mistake with Amir, that Amir was a brave, decent, sensitive boy who was trying to be true to himself, and who was ultimately hurt by what I did.

I start my story like this: "I once had a student who was always very quiet in class, but I could tell that he paid attention. I could tell because he always submitted his homework on time and he did reasonably well in all his assignments. His test results could have been improved, but I can tell when a student is trying his best. He never spoke much to the other students. I got the sense that he was a loner, that he kept to himself, and very much preferred it that way. I never once asked him why this was so. It has never been in my nature to ask sensitive questions like that. Neither did I push him to be more than who he was, although now I wished I had done so. I know these teen years for you boys can be difficult. All of you need time and space to grow and come into your own. I had believed this was the case with this particular student. I also had the sense that none of the other boys paid him much attention either, which was good, as it meant that nobody was bullying him in school, or making him uncomfortable. They left him alone."

The boys have been listening without interrupting me. They can be capricious and ill-disciplined at times, but also sweet. Now they listen patiently to the ramblings of this aging teacher. There is a real sense of affection and respect emanating from them, I like to believe, lasting for just this very moment. Usually they get restless after just ten minutes of hearing me speak. But then again, I am now talking to them about one of their own, or somebody who *used* to be one of them. Maybe there is a boy in this class right now, maybe one of the more silent and invisible ones, who is exactly like Amir. Maybe what I am narrating might reach his ears and sink deep into his mind. Perhaps my words may even offer some genuine comfort, letting him know that he is not the first to experience what Amir went through. I am still a teacher today, I remind myself. And a teacher is supposed to impart more than just knowledge to students; a teacher should inspire individuality and the courage to nourish that individuality. Surely I have done this. Surely I have been a good teacher overall and made my life-changing mark on my boys. So what if this is my last day? I can still make one last difference before I leave this profession behind me.

Amir...As I speak...about Amir, an image of him is becoming clearer. Out of a sea of boys' faces past and present, his face slowly sifts through and pushes to the surface of my thoughts with increasing and nearly overwhelming clarity. His face and his life; the little that I knew about his life, the little that he told me, and the little that eventually became more than I could handle.

It was just after the final exams in the second year of Amir's secondary school life. All the boys had only about two and a half weeks of school left before another long year-end school break. For everyone, holiday plans and trips with families abroad had been arranged and air tickets bought. The atmosphere in the staff room that late afternoon was slightly hectic. The teachers were all making time in their individual schedules to mark their classes' examination scripts. They wanted to get all the necessary marking done in as few days as possible. Piles of green scripts were stacked up on all the teachers' tables. Some were trying to fit them into thick folders so that they could bring them home to mark over the weekend, although the school frowned on this practice. I intended to read my boys' scripts in school during the first week of the holidays, when I could be totally alone to do my marking in peace. Marks only had to be recorded into the school's system by the end of the school holidays, but most teachers wanted to do this long before then, so they could enjoy their holidays. I wanted to take my time; I hated to rush through something as important as marking a student's exam paper. Then after entering all my students' marks into the system, I had made plans with Christopher to take a leisurely vacation to Vietnam for a week, then maybe even a trip to Cambodia or Laos for another few days.

I was thinking about all these things at my corner desk in the bustling staff room when I decided to step out for a moment. I wanted to take a break from thinking about work and stroll along the common corridor, when I noticed one of my students at the far end; he did not dare come closer to the staff room as students were firmly not allowed to come inside or loiter outside during marking time. Now he had spotted me and was wondering how to greet me from so far away. I decided to make it easier for him by striding over quickly. The boy's white uniform was slightly tucked out over his brown pants, but I decided I would not mention it once he came closer. It was coming to the last few days of the school year and I did not want to ruin anybody's holiday mood.

"Afternoon, Mrs de Souza," Amir greeted me sheepishly, just as I was approaching him. "I was...waiting around here hoping to see you before you go home."

"Afternoon, Amir," I answered, looking around to see if there were any boys other than Amir coming to see me. I thought that perhaps a whole group of them was waiting somewhere nearby to ask me questions about the exams that they had just taken. "What are you still doing here in school?"

"Er...I was wondering if I could talk to you about something. I don't really know who else to turn to. I thought maybe after the exams would be a good time. And I can't talk to my classmates. I'm not sure the others would...would be interested in what I have to say. I just wouldn't feel good telling them."

I stared at him more closely now. He looked uncomfortable, even a little upset by something. He must have been standing at this corner of the corridor for some time, waiting for me, contemplating whether to give up waiting or not, whether talking to me was even a good idea. He was trying his best not to show his sense of discomfort. I also noticed that his hair had previously been a crew cut but was slowly growing out. There was one tiny bead of sweat glistening at the corner of his forehead. He smelled vaguely of sweat, although it was not an entirely unpleasant smell. The boy looked like he smiled a lot whenever he felt uncomfortable, as he was smiling now, somewhat awkwardly. I also thought that if he smiled more broadly and genuinely, it would actually be an appealing and attractive smile.

"Well," I said, thinking back on the scripts sitting on my table in the staff room, before turning my attention more fully back to Amir. He looked like he had something serious to say, something that required some significant amount of time for him to explain. "How about we have a cup of tea at the school canteen then. Would that be all right with you? Then you can tell me what's on your mind."

"Okay, Mrs de Souza," Amir replied, gratefully.

At the canteen, all the stall-owners were already packing up their things to go home, so Amir and I simply bought our steaming beverages from a vending machine at a far end of the canteen and sat with our paper cups, warm and heavy with tea, at the nearest table we could find. None of the other boys or teachers in the school were inclined to hang about the canteen at this hour, so it was almost empty.

"All right, Amir," I said, raising my cup to venture a sip, trying to keep my tone and the mood of the conversation casual. "What's on your mind?"

Amir studied his own steaming cup for a short while. I could tell that he was gathering courage, or finding the right words, before deciding to speak. At this moment, I remembered another incident with another boy just a year before, when he had come to tell me that his parents were leaving the country to work overseas, and that they were going to take him with them. The boy (I vaguely recalled that Jeffrey was his name, although I could have been wrong) had wanted to see me and thank me for being such a kind teacher. It was always gratifying to be reminded that I had done a praiseworthy job as an educator, especially when there were times I doubted my own capabilities. If I remembered correctly, Jeffrey had never really been an outstanding student; not lazy, just not a particularly good student; much like Amir, I gathered. He was a Chinese boy, about the same height as Amir, but more plump. I must have encouraged Jeffrey and spent a little more time on him than on the better students, ensuring that he understood and absorbed more than he thought he himself had been capable of in class.

I did tend to remember better the faces and names of students who had done more than the minimum in my classes or on their tests and final exams. Unfortunately, there had been too many boys in my years of teaching who were the type to merely scrape by. This was not to say that the poorer boys had not worked diligently—some of them worked very hard, a few naturally more than others—but it did not mean that they could fully absorb whatever it was that they were trying to learn. Just because one worked hard in class, did not mean that they would automatically become a straight-A student. Life could be unfair like that. It was an unfortunate truth that some boys were just brighter sparks than others. I felt sorry for the less capable boys. They lived in a fast-paced and developed country that prided itself on being fiercely meritocratic. Such boys would (at most) just get by in such a social system. And God help them if they wanted to start a big family, buy a home for themselves, etc., in the future. In a way, I had been glad when I heard Jeffrey would be moving to another country to live and study. I had heard that students like Jeffrey generally tended to do better at school in countries like Australia or even the States, where competition amongst students was simply not as stressful; not that I could remember where it was Jeffrey and his family had eventually relocated in the end. Watching Amir stare into his paper cup, I wondered if Amir had ever contemplated moving somewhere else.

Amir looked up finally and told me what was on his mind. "Mrs de Souza, I'm not really sure why I think you're somebody who would understand what I'm about to say. I just have this hunch about you, that's all. And anyway, there's really nobody else that I can turn to. There's nobody else who wouldn't judge or make fun of me, I guess. You see, I've been having these *feelings* since, I don't know, around Primary Six, I think, and I'm not sure what I'm supposed to do about them. I can't talk to my father about it, because...because I know he wouldn't understand. I can't talk to my friends because, well, because they'd only tease me. They might even stop being my friends. I know because I hear them making fun of other people using those words."

"What words, Amir?" I asked. I felt flattered that Amir had turned to me to talk about his problems. I had never quite thought of myself as approachable enough to be anyone's confidante. I knew that my boys saw me as detached and formal, yet hopefully not entirely cold and unfriendly. That was the general image of myself that I had always tried to project anyway. I felt honoured that Amir could see something more beyond my self-possessed exterior.

Then I recalled that Amir's mother had died in a car crash many years ago, and he had only his father and paternal grandmother staying with him at home. I wondered why I had not remembered this before? It was the school principal, Mr Ong (a fifty-something-year-old Chinese man with a protruding belly and an oily face), who had informed me about this when Amir first appeared in my class. Amir's father had personally thanked the principal in his office for allowing Amir to move up to the next academic level. That was when Amir's father had also told Mr Ong about their situation at home, hoping to gain extra sympathy points for Amir. Amir had only barely gotten by with passes in his examination scores; just a few marks off and he would have failed many of his important subjects.

Amir paused for a long time before he continued talking. "What words? Faggot, *pondan*, *ah kua*...I think I'm gay, Mrs de Souza."

I became silent for a moment. This was the first time anyone had ever confessed anything like this to me. I was not quite sure how to react. Being in an all-boys school, matters about sexuality had to arise sooner or later, yet I had not expected that any boy would trust me with such an intimate aspect of himself. Also, I personally did not have any friends who were gay. I had little clue about what being gay entailed beyond a few things I had read about in books or magazines.

"Well, er...Amir, how do you know? I mean, how do you know, for sure? And have you known for a long time?" I asked. I was stalling for time, so that I could think about how I could properly handle the situation, while at the same time trying to seem open-minded and understanding.

I was certain I had never known any gays in my life. None of my friends from school when I was growing up; there *had* been rumours about a few classmates in the convent school where I had studied, rumours about girls doing peculiar things with other girls, but I had never thought much about such rumours. I had simply dismissed them as malicious lies. School was such a strange time for both boys and girls at that age, a phase when they had to deal with hormonal changes inflicted by puberty, as well as the cruel politics of clique formations and peer pressure. I had also heard about a few local celebrities on television and in the movies who were supposedly non-heterosexual, but I had never thought long and hard about the subject. I had never even discussed the matter with Christopher; I wondered if he had ever met with students who confided in him regarding their sexualities.

Amir looked more uncomfortable now, as though regretting his decision to talk to me about this topic. I decided to allay his fears. "Look here, it's quite all right. You can talk to me about this. I won't judge. It's not as if you're causing any harm to anyone by being who you are, right? Just keep talking to me. Don't be embarrassed. I'm here to help—and to listen."

As I am relating a much-shortened version of this story to my students, quickly summing up the conversation with Amir while excluding key details that might point to Amir's sexuality, couching it implicitly in such terms as 'a private issue' or 'a crisis of identity' (leading some boys in class to turn to each other now, wondering openly about what this 'crisis' could be about; I can even hear a repressed snicker at the back of the room, issued probably by Subra, which makes me glad I have chosen to leave out much from my story), I am privately unsure if what I am recalling now is what I actually said in response to Amir. Yet it sounds just about right. Maybe I actually said something more curt and less pleading in response to Amir and do not want to admit it; perhaps I am dressing up the truth to make myself look better in this situation. Upon rapid and closer inspection of the past, I think that I *must* have said something positive and encouraging to Amir, because he continued talking, didn't he? The boy did relent and reveal everything to me about his secret, inner life.

"I've known for a while now," Amir was saying. "Maybe since two years ago, when I started having...certain dreams or fantasies about other boys in school...when I even sometimes thought I could be in *love* with them."

"But maybe it's just a phase. Have you thought about that?"

"No, Mrs de Souza. It's not a phase. I *know* it's not a phase. Boys my age have fantasies about girls. They want to do certain things with girls. I'm not interested at all in girls. I don't like them, not in that way, not at all. I know what I like, Mrs de Souza. You must believe me. I don't like girls at all."

Amir's insistence was jarring to my ears. I wanted to engage with him in a logical and rational way. It also occurred to me that maybe the more responsible thing to do would be to recommend that Amir speak to somebody more knowledgeable than me regarding this subject. Thinking about such a recommendation helped me to extricate myself from a growing sense of discomfort in dealing with Amir's problem now. "Don't take this the wrong way, Amir, but why are you telling me all this? Maybe you would prefer to speak to the school counsellor? Why me, Amir?"

Now it was my last question to Amir that sounded jarring to my own ears. I sounded like a child whining. It was not how a teacher was supposed to sound when a student was asking her for help.

"The school counsellor wouldn't understand. Have you seen him, Mrs de Souza? He reminds me of the boys in class, you know, like an older version of my classmates, the kind who likes sports and girls and all those things I don't like, those things that I could never like, even if I tried. The type who'd only make fun of me if he knew the truth about me. I know he'd try to be nice and all, but he'd only be pretending. I'd be able to tell if he'd pretend to listen to me without really making fun of me secretly. I thought maybe *you* would understand better, since you're a woman..."

I was not sure whether to be flattered or to point out that this was a potentially sexist thing to say. I decided on neither. Maybe he was right. Maybe women were indeed more sensitive in dealing with such issues.

"Amir, I'm going to tell you right now that I'm quite shocked by what you're telling me. It's not that I disapprove of what you're saying; please don't think that. I just...I'm just not sure what to say. You see, I've never really met any gay people in my life. I'm not even fully sure what it means to be gay. I know I'm so much older than you, and I know that what you're going through must be challenging, but I haven't had the opportunity in my life to meet, well, somebody like you."

"Mrs de Souza, it really isn't anything special," replied Amir, in a tone that was surprisingly lucid and direct for a change. "When I first knew about these feelings, I went to the public library in my neighbourhood—not our school library; sorry, Teacher, but our library is really useless—and found as many books as I could about being gay. Some people say we are born this way. Others say we are brought up to become gay. A lot of people, including me, think it is a bit of both. But it's also simple: being gay just means I like other boys; while lesbians just like other girls. It's only 'difficult' because *other* people force us to see this as something difficult. They want us to change. They want us to be just like them. They need us to be 'normal' because they don't understand how somebody can like somebody else from the same sex."

It was strange to hear Amir talk about this, and for him to utter 'sex' in a conversation with his much-older and obviously conservative English teacher, a female adult who might even be older than Amir's own father. Amir obviously felt uncomfortable again, because he was looking down shyly at his cup, from which he had not yet taken a single sip.

"Drink your tea, Amir," I reminded him, "before it gets cold."

Amir quietly and nervously did as he was told. His drink was probably lukewarm, as he managed to gulp it down until his cup was half empty.

"I've heard about the things that you have mentioned," I went on. "Not that I've read much about the topic, and not that I can pretend to ever understand it for myself. But it must be much more complicated than what you've said, Amir. It's illegal to be gay, for example, in this country. I've read this in the newspapers. Do you know that, Amir? You could go to jail, you know, for...doing certain things with another man. I need to warn you about this because it *is* a very real concern."

"Yes, I know. But I'm sure the police don't really want to catch anybody for doing something private like that. How can they when there are so many homosexuals in this country? You don't really hear about police catching gays for doing it, right? Or maybe they do, but that is because they do things with each other in a park or in the public toilets or something like that. I'm sure things are changing here, Mrs de Souza. Things must be getting better. I'm sure we're becoming more open-minded and more accepting. There are just too many of us. The police can't possibly be arresting *all* of us, right?"

"Amir, maybe they just don't report it much, have you thought about that? Maybe they want to downplay the publicity, but in actual fact they're really arresting people for being gay on a regular basis, for doing things that are still considered against the law. Have you thought about that?"

"So Mrs de Souza, are you telling me you don't approve of anyone being gay?"

"No, Amir, no, no, not at all. That's not what I'm saying at all. I know I sound like I disapprove, but I'm just, well, I'm only letting you know it can be dangerous to be gay in this country. I don't want to have to see your face in the papers or something awful like that. You're such a good boy, Amir; you don't deserve to go to jail or be publicly humiliated for being who you are! I'm sure you don't want that too, right?"

"I know, Mrs de Souza. But it's not going to stop me, or stop us, from being who we are. We can't help who we are. And like you said, it's not as if I'm causing any harm to anyone else, right?"

"Don't take this the wrong way, but...have you heard of homosexuals who have maybe tried *not* being gay, and maybe turned their lives around?" As I said this, I realised how hysterical and small-minded I sounded. I was not a repressed Catholic nun, for goodness' sake! But I felt as if I had to say these things, or at least play the devil's advocate in this situation. What if being gay was just a phase for Amir? What then? Amir was almost a year away from turning sixteen. When he stepped over that threshold into adulthood, might he change his mind about this part of himself? I did not want him to make a mistake (energised by my possible encouragement) that he could regret later. For certain, offering a different perspective *had* to be the responsible thing to do.

"And please don't think that I am talking as somebody who is religious or closed-minded," I continued. "I know you must come from a Muslim household so I'm not trying to offend you by saying this. I'm really the least religious person I know. I mean how can I possibly believe in God when God was not there to help my Christopher through his cancer and his horrible pain, pain that I know he suffered even though he pretended the cancer didn't hurt him at all—"

My thoughts stop in their tracks with a feeling like a nasty jolt, like jamming the brakes when the car has been moving too quickly whilst trying to avoid a pedestrian pushing a pram across the street. I am mixing up memories here, confusing one version of what I said to Amir with an altogether different recollection of what I felt when I watched Christopher battle his illness: Christopher in his blue gown, lying on his stiff hospital bed; the nurses sauntering back and forth outside along the corridor, indifferent to my husband's discomfort; Christopher with his eyes closed as he tried to distance himself from the pain; the cancer spreading from his pancreas all over his body, cell by agonising cell; I was sitting there beside him, watching as he seemed to *will* his pain into submission.

This later memory is encroaching on my recounting of what I said to Amir in the canteen. I had certainly not said any of these things about Christopher to Amir, or now to the boys in the classroom who are still listening to my account about this unnamed student with his special 'crisis of identity'. I certainly did not mention anything about God. I would never touch on sensitive issues like religion in front of any student in this way. Some aspect of my confusion must have manifested as a break in my flow of speech because I find myself staring blankly at the boys in my classroom now, having halted in the middle of a sentence.

Instead what I said to Amir *must* have gone something like this: "I'm really the least religious person I know. And I certainly pride myself on being progressive and liberal. I'm just worried that what you're going through might just be a phase in your life when you're only experimenting with... sexual matters. I don't want you to make a decision now that you might regret later in life. Have you ever wondered, perhaps, whether your feelings might change over time? Have you thought that maybe you could change from being... totally gay?"

"No," Amir replied, resolutely. "No, I cannot change. Can *you* change, Mrs de Souza? Could you suddenly like women in that way? Could you suddenly like doing *those* kinds of things with other women?"

Amir was angry, and his anger was giving him the courage to challenge me. I had always prided myself on being glad that my students had the ability to speak their minds, even if what they said could be contrary to my own opinions. On the one hand, I was glad to hear that spark in Amir's voice. On the other hand, I still believed I had to continue down this road in antagonising him. I am not even sure now why I felt convinced that this was the right thing to do.

Yet something held me back in that instant. Something told me that going down that tract was ultimately futile, even potentially wrong. Also, Amir had asked me something frightfully personal: had I ever had feelings for another woman? The answer was a firm *no*, ringing loudly in my skull. But once the ringing subsided, I wondered: what was really so ominous about dwelling upon that question? A few faces from the past drifted into my mind from my convent school, then later from my university days, women whom I had considered exceptionally attractive. How deeply did such instances of attraction truly run? I had met Christopher early in my university life. We had fallen in love. We had been drawn, sexually attracted, to each other, without any iota of doubt. Maybe my love for Christopher had eclipsed other niggling feelings at the back of my mind, feelings that when left unconsidered, had simply fizzled out and become extinct. Just because those feelings had disappeared, it did not mean that they had not been there, maybe once or twice: a spark, a flickering star.

"I see your point, Amir. I'm sorry for talking like this to you. I guess I feel that it's my role to say these things to you. You're still young. I need to make you aware of the consequences of your actions. I need to help you see alternative perspectives, viewpoints that might go against what you know. It's so important that you see the whole picture, because if you miss out on one part of the picture, you might regret it later in your life. Seeing the whole picture will help you to make an informed decision regarding this matter. Don't you agree?"

"But I *have* thought about these things, Mrs de Souza. You think I've not thought about these things? I think about these things all the time! I think about them even when I'm trying to sleep! Who actually makes a choice like this, thinking that they would be happy *choosing* to be gay? It's a horrible thing, you know, to be gay. Suddenly you become aware that everybody might hate you. Your friends could stop talking to you; people would start thinking you are a freak, and start calling your names behind your back. I wonder how many boys in this macho shithead missionary school are actually gay and are just not willing to talk about it because they're afraid of being made fun of, afraid of being hated for life, afraid of being ignored."

Amir's voice was rising in volume. But realising that he had said 'shithead' in front of his English teacher piped him down a notch. He was abruptly embarrassed that he had used that word. He became visibly more conscious and reflective about how much he had already told me until this point, wondering now if he was doing the right thing in talking to me.

To my credit, I chose to ignore the fact that Amir had swore. "Wait, Amir. Hold on, I'm glad you're telling me all this. Please don't for one second regret that you've told me these personal things about yourself. I want to try and understand what you're going through. I really do. It's good to talk about it, and not bottle it all up inside. The worst thing you can do is keep these things buried inside you. Such things can eat at you over time, and drive you mad, or poison you and turn you into a monster. Amir, we all live in a country where so many things get bottled up inside ourselves. In fact, we're regularly encouraged to keep our demons hidden. There's still so much censorship here. There are so many things that we cannot say in public, as if saying such things would invite chaos into our society. We're encouraged to be polite all the time, even when our politeness is usually not real and skin-deep at best. So I'm glad, so glad, that you're talking, and talking to me right here and now. I'm here to listen to you; I'm here for you, Amir.

Please believe me—and keep on talking."

"I know. I'm glad you're here, listening. I really don't have anyone else to turn to. I don't know if anyone else in this school has the same problem in having nobody else to talk to about this, having nobody who would understand."

"Maybe you're braver than everyone else in this school then. That's an excellent first step, you know. Just to be brave, and to be able to talk about it. So what if people reject you afterwards? People are always rejecting each other for some silly reason or other. People are so often unkind, or they get so busy that they forget to be kind to each other, especially here in this country. We pay so much lip-service to being kind, but nobody is really kind. Haven't you felt that way? We are all too busy looking after ourselves, looking after our own interests."

"Wow, Mrs de Souza, I didn't know you felt that way about people."

"Well, not *everyone* is like this, Amir. I'm sure not everybody in the world is like this. I'm just talking about this place we're living in. The ways people here behave on the roads these days. How people here are so caught up in keeping their jobs, in being cool or different or wealthy, rushing always from one place to another, seeming to appear connected to the rest of the world, to be famous in one way or another. I don't know. Maybe I'm exaggerating everything. Maybe I'm being unnecessarily pessimistic. But I think we live in a city where people are really not nice at all. Most people here like to believe that they're good people, that they're nice and decent, but no one is, really. Do you ever get that feeling, Amir?"

This time, as I recollect and summarise this part of

the conversation for my classroom full of boys seemingly enthralled by my story and still irrepressibly curious about Amir's hidden conflict (from the way I have been relating my story so far, they must think that it has something to do with Amir's religious beliefs instead of his sexual preferences), I am no longer certain if I said any of this to Amir. I know that the actual story that I have been telling is a collage of bits and pieces of what actually happened, with more than just real names and private issues left out from my sharply shortened account. I do not even reveal that I might or might not have expressed opinions like "people are really not nice at all". But the truth is important. Or the *essence* of the truth has to be kept intact. I am committing a huge injustice to Amir if I neglect to preserve the essence of these memories, the deeper, authentic truth linking these memories about how I tried to help him, and the consequences of my efforts.

I also have to stop mixing personal sentiments in the present with memories from the past. I might feel this way today about how people are generally unkind in this country, but surely I did not feel this way all those years ago, especially not during the time Amir came to chat with me. I was a different human being then. I was more idealistic, more hopeful. Perhaps all I said to Amir was this: "Maybe you're just braver than everyone else in sticking to what you believe in. It's good to be brave. It's an excellent first step to being a mature and thinking adult." This is the version of my response that I tell the boys in my classroom now, practically word for word. Yes, such a response sounds more like the younger, optimistic and cheery version of me from those years ago.

I realised Amir was being silent again. I wanted to fill the silence and so I kept talking. "Maybe I know nothing about what you're going through, Amir. But I do know that talking things out really helps us to understand ourselves better. There can be nothing worse than keeping things to yourself until you blow up one day in ways you don't expect."

Amir then replied in a manner that sounded like he was trying to make a joke (Instead of revealing what he actually said, I simply sum up his response to my class as "he said something sarcastic in return, but I know he was only expressing his private frustration."). "Maybe I might end up getting married to a woman I don't love, and have lots of children, and infect all of them with my unhappiness because I wasn't true to myself years ago, because I gave in to the pressure to fit in with this stupid society."

The word 'infect' was a needle sliding into my brain. It was hard to hear that steely bite of resentment in his voice without cringing. Amir was still so young, too young to sound so bitter. I spoke quickly: "I hope that *that* will never happen to you, Amir. Please, please do not grow up with bitterness and regret. That's the worse thing that could happen to someone like you. You deserve so much better for yourself. You deserve to be true to who you are. You deserve to be *happy* for the rest of your life."

Amir's expression showed he was glad I had said this. "Thanks, Mrs de Souza."

I then imagined that in the following year, when Amir would come back to join my class, I might not be able to look at him in the same way again. I would always be on eggshells around him; I might even avoid asking him questions in class, for fear of hurting him. Maybe it was not necessarily a bad thing, being careful with a student's feelings in this way.

Amir picked up his cup and gulped down the remaining tea inside. I used the opportunity to take a drink too, slowly sipping while thinking about what I was going to say next.

After Amir put down his empty cup, he looked at me somewhat appreciatively and said: "I want to thank you, Mrs de Souza. For being such a kind teacher, and a great listener. You're the nicest teacher in this school. Seriously."

It was an abrupt thing to say. I was not sure whether Amir was just saying this so he could round up our conversation as soon as possible, but I was nonetheless moved by what Amir had expressed. Had I really made some positive impact in the life of this student? I still felt that the conversation could not be over so soon. Surely I could say something more useful than what I had already said. I had to round off this conversation in a much more revelatory way. After all, I had not really given him any concrete advice that he could use. I tried to think hard about what valuable, life-changing advice I could give. There had to be something I could offer that would truly and ultimately help.

I strived to be more honest, hoping that my honesty would help to heal that wound within Amir, an injury that I might have accidentally opened further through our conversation. "I wish there was something more I could say to help, Amir. I've not known you to be such a...sensitive boy. You've always been so quiet in class, but now that I know these crucial things about you, I want to ask about where you wish to go from here.

What happens now? Are you maybe able to make gay friends outside of school, since you cannot make such friends here? Other gays who can help you? I wish I knew someone who had the relevant life experience to talk to you more insightfully about these matters. I do think I've been incredibly useless today, talking to you now."

"No, no, Mrs de Souza. You've been a great help, really. I'm just glad that I was able to tell you about myself. Like you said, talking helps, especially now. School has been tough. The exams were...difficult. I'm not sure how well I will do next year."

"Well, don't give up on school! As your teacher, I can assure you that I will always be there if you need the extra help. I'm sure the other teachers are glad to help you too, if you ask them. I'm sure they could also offer a listening ear, if you asked."

I was actually not too sure about this last bit. I was uncertain if any of the other teachers were like me. In fact, I doubted if any of the other teachers would have handled this confession by Amir in the way that I had just handled it. For sure, many of the other teachers would have been far more adamant that Amir change his ways, or even that he turn to religion and even psychiatry to repress who he was.

How I despised organised religions. I reveal some gist of this segue in my thoughts to my students in the middle of my story about Amir: Christopher and I used to have long discussions about how religion or religious beliefs were turning out *not* to be forces of good in the world; how, for example, the Catholic Church was driving up cases of HIV infections in Africa because of an insistence on abstinence and the banning of condoms; how religions divided people more than they brought people together, such as how the Buddhists were treating the Rohingya Muslims in Burma; or that eternal strife between Israel and Palestine, driven by both religious as well as cultural differences. I tell my boys that Christopher and I used to have such intelligent and open conversations about a whole range of philosophical and political topics, not always agreeing on everything but still eager to talk things through until we were both tired out from such discussions. In fact, we had a similar exchange about the value of religion when I was in hospital with him in between his treatments. Such long and lively conversations helped to distract my husband from bouts of nausea and his unwavering sense of bodily discomfort.

In the last week at the hospital before Christopher succumbed to his cancer, we talked a lot about practical and immediate matters, making sure his will was in order, ensuring that his money would go to me after he was gone. We talked about the meaning of life, whether life carried on after death; for Christopher, the question had no certain answer, and as such, he insisted that to discuss it further would be an act of futility. I believe, however, that there is something like a soul that exists within the folds and sinews of the flesh; like the Hindus, I believe that the soul is probably very small, thumb-sized, a bauble of light. But I am not convinced about reincarnation. I am also not convinced by what the monotheistic religions have to say about the soul, and how it exists so that it can be redeemed in the course of one's life through prayer or faith. I believe that, upon death, the soul passes from one's corpse into an ocean of light from which all things come, but I refuse to relate that metaphorical ocean to notions like Yahweh or Brahma. That light is bigger, more infinite, than all of these man-made concepts combined. Affectionately, Christopher called me "a hopeful, irreligious, new-age dreamer". I did not disagree. How could I disagree with a smiling man in a hospital bed with an intravenous drip running out from his thinning arm? How could I disagree with a dying man I both loved and pitied?

I am remembering such conversations with my husband, relating parts of what I can remember to my class now (instead of carrying on more germanely about Amir) when, against my will, my eyes wander to the school field outside the classroom again, while the boys wait for me to carry on speaking, some of them exchanging surreptitious looks; perhaps they are moved (if such young boys can be moved) by what I have said about my late husband; maybe they are even reflective (anything is possible with these students) about what I have argued about organised religions. There is nobody on the field outside. Sunlight has drawn fresh shadows across different parts of that rectangular patch of grass. There is no sign of Christopher anywhere. My boys must wonder if perhaps their teacher is spacing out again. I have to return to my story.

I talk about what Amir said after I told him that I would always be there to help him, academically or otherwise.

"I appreciate all that you're saying, Mrs de Souza. I really do," said Amir.

But I could tell that this boy had more on his mind, so I decided to drag on the conversation. "It's not a problem,

Amir. If you'd like to talk about anything else, you can carry on talking, if you like."

"No, no, really...there's nothing else. I just, like you said, needed to talk, that's all. That's all."

An awkward silence fell between us. The canteen was completely empty now. There were no boys hanging about. The last school bell must have already rung, even though, caught up in our little exchange, neither Amir nor I had heard it. The daylight was dimming and soon the canteen's fluorescent lights would flicker on automatically. It dawned upon me then that I would probably be teaching in this school for the rest of my life. I was not sure how or why I understood this as an unshakeable truth. It was, at best, a premonition of the future, an irrational prediction. (I expect to hear Subra saying at this point, rather sardonically, "Well, you were right, Mrs de Souza." For some reason, he does not grab the opportunity to make any remark.) Ever since I was a girl, I had always dreamed of becoming a teacher. The teachers of my past had been poised and formal, but severe, educators who brooked no disobedience; yet they had also been kind and caring towards attentive students like me. I guess it was that sense of balance between severity and compassion, that immovable core of mental discipline, which I had admired most, and which I'd wanted to cultivate within myself growing up.

Not that it had been difficult for any teacher to like me as a young student. I was sure I had been an excellent and sensitive student. With my father always in a foreign country doing business, and mother waiting grumpily at home, waiting for her only daughter to come back so she could lecture me about everything that was wrong with being a housewife, with being stuck and bored all the time and how lucky it was that my father got to gallivant to distant and exotic places, it was not surprising how I *loved* being in school. I had not made friends easily, being shy and withdrawn from an early age, but I had loved to read and study and lose myself in the school library. Teachers loved to teach me and have me in their classes because I always gave the right responses; how I loved to put up my hand, eager to answer questions when nobody else would. At the same time, I knew I was never arrogant and was always well-mannered when I answered my teachers' questions.

While in the canteen with Amir, I gazed about at the old colonial architecture of the central building, with its aura of the past bleeding into the ever-changing present, which no amount of repeated paint jobs could remove entirely, the spacious classrooms with their high ceilings, and the abstract (and sometimes ugly, depending on the time of day and the position of the sun) sculptures dotting the gardens around the assembly courtyard that had existed since the country was under British rule, all of these aspects of the school compound giving the institution an atmosphere that was at once haughtily 'old-world' but also nostalgically and reassuringly familiar and timeless. Amir was staring into the empty cup on the table before him, then he looked up towards a point above my left shoulder, analysing something beyond me. I liked to think that perhaps Amir was gazing into the future at that moment. He could have been seeing himself as an adult outside of this school, somebody who already lived beyond the heartache of self-hatred and the trials and terrors of rejection and social marginalisation. What would Amir look like as a fully grown man? Would he be taller and better looking, with more hair on his head, and retaining that increasingly enigmatic smile? Would he still be Muslim? Where would he be working, and would his colleagues know about his sexuality? Would such things matter in the future, whether one was gay or not? Would he still be living in this country, and with his aging father? Or would his father be dead by then, like his grandmother? A dead man would no longer be able to pass judgements on his son, right? Or would Amir be living and working overseas, where he would have found a supportive community of fellow gay friends? Was Amir thinking about all these things in the span of those few seconds?

Amir spoke again, looking only now and then into my eyes; this time he spoke without stopping: "I'm feeling lost, Mrs de Souza. I know I've said that gays can't help who they are, but I do wish I wasn't gay. I wish I didn't like boys, that I didn't like men. I wish I was normal like everyone else. I hate being different. There's nothing special about being different, not like this. I was brought up as a Muslim. My father's a religious man, and so is my grandmother. I'll never get married. I'd never be able to live with myself, knowing I got married to please my father and my relatives. I'd never want to have any children, because if one of my children grew up and turned out to be gay, I wouldn't want him or her to think about the things that I'm thinking about now, to feel the things I'm feeling now. I wouldn't want my children to suffer like how I'm suffering. I wouldn't want any of them to be made fun of when other people find out. And what would happen if my children found out that their father was secretly gay? What would they think of me then? Would they blame me? Would they hate me?

"I know this sounds horrible but I'm glad at least my mother is dead. If Allah exists, I hope he's right now pressing his big hands on my mother's eyes and ears in heaven, so she can never hear what I'm telling you today. Do you know, Mrs de Souza, I remember every little mean thing my father has ever said about people on television or people in real life, when he suspected that these people were gay, or even if they were just a little bit effeminate. My father is *mean*, Mrs de Souza. How would he react if he ever found out? And my grandmother. I...really want her to pass away soon. She's very, very old, so there's a high chance this will happen in the next few years. I *want* it to happen. Like my father, my grandmother wants to see me married. If my mother was alive, she would have wanted me to get married too. My grandma talks about seeing me married with children all the time. She talks to all my relatives about what a wonderful father I would make if I got married and if I had lots and lots of stupid children.

"Imagine me married, my pretty wife in her tudung, my little children, all my proper Muslim family at the mosque on Fridays, saying hello to everyone as if there is nothing wrong, as if we're all perfectly happy. Do you know I have many, many dreams at night about this? I keep dreaming about my future wife and my family. I dream about what it would be like if one day they found out I really didn't care about them, that everything had been a lie. I dream about what their faces would look like after they find out, or after I've told them. I dream a lot, Mrs de Souza. I always dream in colour and the dreams, if they aren't wet dreams, they're very seldom happy."

Amir took a deep breath. I was stunned. It had not taken much for Amir to speak his mind. And he had so much left to say! In my classroom, as I struggle with how best to sum up Amir's spiel (deciding ultimately to omit much of it in my retelling), I think the only thing I tell my class which is straight out of Amir's mouth is how his dreams were 'seldom happy'. What I was thinking at this point after Amir's rant was that maybe depression was the reason he was speaking like this, and the reason he was not doing as well as he could in his studies. Depression was not something that anyone could easily crawl out from. Bouts of depression came and went, as unpredictable as rain, and always came back.

Amir, noticing that his English teacher was not saying anything, became embarrassed again. "I'm sorry, Mrs de Souza. I didn't mean to be rude or anything..."

"No, no, Amir. It's completely fine," I quickly interjected. "I'm glad. No, I'm actually, really, really relieved to hear you talk to me like this."

In my mind, I had the certain thought that I would never pick on him to answer a question in class ever again; I would never want such a blow-up like this in my classroom if ever Amir felt that he was about to explode emotionally. How would I deal with it if this happened during any of my lessons? Would I be able to send him to the principal's office to be disciplined, after knowing so much about Amir's private turmoil? Then I felt guilty, even ashamed. Where was my sense of professionalism? Where was my compassion? Was it so difficult to distinguish personal concerns from school-related matters? How could I believe that I would not be able to teach Amir while, at the same time, act as his listening ear whenever he needed me to hear him out?

And what would happen after secondary school was over for Amir? Would he come back to visit me in the staff room? Would I be able to find time to listen to Amir's troubles? There was a high chance that it would probably never happen. Amir would have moved on by then from the angry, self-pitying boy that he was right now. He would want to put this shameful part of his past behind him or pretend it never happened. All students eventually move on from such dizzying emotional states when they leave school, when the messiness and pragmatic realities of life finally catch up with them.

Compared to Amir, I realised that I myself had never had to go through such turmoil as a teenager. Amir's predicament was heartbreaking. How would I have handled it if I had known, at Amir's present age, that I was sexually inclined in a different way from other girls in my school? Would I have been able to confront the truth? Would I have been able to discuss such matters with my parents—my distant father and irritable, garrulous mother?

But I knew that by dwelling on myself now, I was half-consciously trying to escape from this present moment because I was afraid Amir's emotional outburst was becoming too much for me to bear. I had to come back to the present. I had to tackle Amir's troubles head-on. What kind of teacher and human being would I be if I ran away from a student's emotional pain like this, especially after this person, this sensitive and vulnerable boy, had confessed so much? Surely a student like Amir, after he had revealed so much, would also become a friend? I had responsibilities to fulfil, not just as a teacher now. The line in my head that separated the role of educator from the role of a confidante had become irrevocably blurred.

Next time in class, I would just have to be more alert to changes in Amir's mood. If there was a dark cloud hanging about him, I would simply avoid asking him anything during the lesson, so as not to draw any attention to him from the other boys, and then after school I would ask to talk privately to him, drawing him out from his shell. I would get him to open himself up to the world again.

I became conscious that I had not said anything for a while. Amir was observing me with an anticipatory and almost injured look, fearing that he had created a newly uncomfortable distance between himself and his teacher.

"Amir," I started again. "You never have to apologise to me. There's nothing you need to be sorry for."

Perhaps what I was really wishing at that moment was that I would be able to say something that would fix everything, something that would solve Amir's problems and turn him into a well-adjusted, happy boy, a boy with a happy future. So what if he was gay? Being gay did not mean that he had to suffer from depression. I had an idea. "What if you actually sat down and talked to your father about this? Or why not both of you speak to a counsellor? With your father on your side, you would be able to work through this problem together."

Then I had an even better idea. "Why not," I suggested, "I set up a meeting between me and your father and you could be there too? We could *both* talk to him. What do you think?"

"No!" Amir shouted.

I was taken aback. "But why, Amir?"

"It would never work; my father would never understand! He would think that you're just telling him there's something wrong with his son, and that maybe his son's homosexuality has something to do with him being a bad parent, that it's *his* fault. It wouldn't work at all!"

"But have you even *tried* speaking to him?"

"No, but I know my father. He won't get it. He never will."

"Then what, Amir? Are you going to wait until you finish school, then Junior College, then after university when you find a job, so that you can move out and start a life when you won't have to repress who you are? Do you know how many years of your life you would have wasted being unhappy by then? If you don't start opening up now and accepting who you are, or talking to somebody about it, what makes you think you'll be able to talk about it later? What if you never accept who you are? What kind of adult would you be then? How would you ever learn to be happy if you don't learn to solve your problems now?"

"Mrs de Souza, I'm sorry but maybe this *is* the only way I can do this. You have to know this: my father will never understand. The truth will only make him so angry and hurt and… Please, Mrs de Souza, please drop this idea."

I knew I was being stymied, but I also knew that there was something in what I was saying. I was convinced that

Amir had just never given his father a chance to contemplate the new change in his son, the whole rich, problematic truth about what his son was becoming. As Amir's teacher, I was convinced that Amir's father would at least be willing to listen respectfully and with an open mind to what *I* had to say about his son. I would inform him that there was nothing wrong with Amir; that Amir was an intelligent, brave and good-hearted soul. In fact, Amir's father should even have been proud of his son for learning to confront his private problems in his own courageous way.

Amir was staring at me with a pleading expression, more than a hint of doubt and suspicion in his eyes. I knew that nothing I could say would change Amir's mind. I sighed and smiled, hoping that I was now coming across as conciliatory. "Don't worry, Amir. I won't bring up the subject again."

I decided to round up the conversation. "Amir, I hope talking to me has made you feel better. I hope you feel more able now to accept who you are. You're not alone. You're a good-hearted, intelligent boy. Remember, you can always come back to talk to me if you have any serious doubts about yourself again. Don't doubt yourself! And one day, one day, you'll even meet gay friends, even close ones who will show you that you're not alone in your struggle for self-acceptance, who'll teach you to love yourself. You have to believe me."

I gave Amir what I hoped was a look of genuine optimism.

"Thank you, Mrs de Souza," Amir finally replied. He looked more relieved than convinced. He was observing his hands opening and closing on the table. I thought that perhaps he was smiling a little as he analysed his fingers curling and uncurling around his empty cup. I thought I glimpsed a glimmer of hope in Amir's downturned face.

"You're right, Mrs de Souza," Amir said, at last. "It's good to know I'm not alone. Thank you. Thank you for listening to me. Thank you so much."

CHAPTER 4

THIS IS NEITHER a dream nor a memory of something that happened. It is something in between. I call it a waking dream (not always a 'daydream' exactly, as it does not necessarily happen in the brightness of daylight), something I do in the pauses between sentences, during a break in a lesson when every student is writing and looking down into an exercise book, or in the minutes before I sleep. I allow the waking dream to fill such pauses because it can take me away from the monotony of a full day of teaching. Just a few moments ago, I had such a dream when I saw Christopher in my classroom and then traipsing across the field outside. Such dreams are often derived from real memories, in which the facts of what happened become altered, embellished, heightened, or inexplicably transformed. I wonder if my mind travels on such flights of fancy, using fragments of my past as some kind of springboard, because I have constricted my imagination elsewhere during the humdrum routines of my day; if maybe such flights occur also as a result of something I've failed to address sufficiently in my past, unresolved aspects of me I have half-consciously repressed. Maybe it is just old age that is the cause; I am losing control of my mind. In one such waking dream, one that I had the night after my exchange with Amir (a dream I choose *not* to share now with the boys in my class in the midst of my story about Amir), my mother entered my thoughts.

I was a child in my waking dream. My mother was sitting on the edge of my bed, talking. She sounded so calm that she could have been reading a bedtime story to me. "I was young like you, Rose, and when I was in school, I met a girl who taught me things about my body, Rose. Things your father never learned about how to give a girl pleasure. Your father knows nothing about how to make a woman happy, Rose. Your father…your father's a useless, useless man."

Had she actually said these things? Or were her words pure fantasy on my part? A part of me wanted to record this down in a diary, maybe turn it into fodder for a piece of creative writing later on, even though another part of me recognised that I would never find the time to do this after such flights of my imagination had concluded, with work and real life always getting in my way. If my mother's words were pure fiction, why was I putting such words in her mouth anyway? Sometimes I scare myself with what I can create with my mind. But I convince myself that such fantasies may mean that I am helping to resolve issues within myself, all on my own.

Mother looked so sad in my mind's eye. She was staring at the wall while speaking to me. "The school headmaster caught us in the act at the back of the school field," mother was saying. She sounded too serene and not at all like her usual cantankerous self. "We got suspended from school. And then the war happened, and so school stopped altogether.

And then the school was blown up. So I never saw my good friend again."

Then she turned to face me. "I miss her, you know. She knew what to do with her fingers and her tongue. I miss her so much. I loved the way her tongue tasted too. Your father knows nothing about this; he knows nothing about her. Your father knows nothing about how to make me happy. Your father knows nothing at all. He's never around. How can he know anything when he's never around? And I know what you want to say—" she was turning again away from me to face the wall—"that your mother is a sick woman. That your mother likes girls, that she likes doing sick things with other girls. But I love your father. I just wish he was around more. I wish your father knew how to make me really, really happy."

Why was I imagining this? I had been thinking first about Amir, about what he had told me, about the things I had said in return; hopefully useful things. Was I hoping to remember that my mother had said something about her sexuality to me so I would be better equipped to deal with Amir's predicament in the present? Or had my mother actually confessed such things about herself, which I had forgotten or suppressed since I had been so young at the time? My next instinct was then to look beside me in real life and there was Christopher, fast asleep in the reassuring darkness, snoring lightly. He issued a whistling sound from his nose that sounded like a firework going off on the other side of the world.

Amir's confession had made a deeper impact on me than I had realised or dared to admit to myself. I got up to use the toilet without turning on the bathroom light, for fear of waking my sleeping husband, who needed his rest or else his students would suffer from his irascibility the next day. I tried to remember, as I crept back into bed, if Mother had actually said those things. Her words had been so out of character. My mother had always nagged and scolded, so she could never sound as serene as she did in my imagination. She had also been prone to hysteria, especially when she was complaining about her life or scolding me, or both at once. Trying as hard as I could, while my eyes adjusted to the dark and focused on the bedroom ceiling, I decided it was all wishful thinking, a mostly useless fantasy. My mother had probably never talked about her growing-up days in any particular detail, and especially not in that wistful way; although she had complained quite often about how unhappy my father had made her.

I wondered if my mother had ever truly loved my father. Surely she did at some point, even if their marriage had become merely perfunctory over time, sustained for the sake of preserving an environment of normalcy for their only child. My parents had made sacrifices for my sake. It was, unfortunately, one of the main reasons I had decided not to have kids myself; I had not wanted to give up anything in my own life in order to worry about children. I had not wanted to become as unhappy as my mother. Christopher had not been happy at the start of our courting days about my decision, but I think he grew to accept my point of view, and he learnt (reluctantly, and mostly because he loved me dearly) to live without the hope of ever having offspring.

My little fantasy about my mother must have been the result of guilt over the way I had handled Amir's confession.

I knew that I should have said something more, or done something to reassure Amir better about how everything would work out in the end. How I hated seeing Amir so sad and helpless. I became certain in this moment, as unconsciousness crept over me, that I knew precisely the right thing to do in order to rescue Amir from his gloom and self-hatred. Knowing this helped me to fall asleep without any more thoughts about my mother or about Amir.

"That evening after our revealing talk, I made up my mind about what I was going to do," I continue to narrate, neglecting to mention how the waking dream about my mother might have led to my eventual certainty. A few boys in the class are staring out at the school field, possibly wondering when my monologue will end. Or maybe they are genuinely listening, even if they have chosen not to look my way. Most of the class is still watching me anyway. Many of the boys have been nothing but attentive, more attentive than they would have been if I were to teach them grammar rules or help them spot possible essay questions that might appear in later examinations. I tell myself to be optimistic. Maybe my last hour with these boys is not a complete waste of time.

Yet what if all my years of teaching have been a waste of time? I have certainly pushed up this school's ranking with my ability to rake in excellent marks. But is this all that should be expected of any teacher? I am mentally going off on another tangent again. The boys stare at me expectantly. It is funny how they can keep staring like that, almost blankly, expressionlessly. This classroom scene is now so still that it looks like a nostalgic photograph taken from the school's yearbook, except for the fan spinning frenetically above our heads. The boys are used to me drifting in and out of attention by now, and do nothing to disrupt my reverie. They wait for me to finish my story about Amir. They know that the story, or my heavily edited version of it, must be far from over.

I lean forward in my chair, press my elbows on the table, fold my hands under my chin this time, and prepare to speak again over the now-forgotten mountain of cards and flowers stacked up before me.

CHAPTER 5

"I NEVER HAD another one-on-one conversation with this student of mine again."

After our conversation, Amir behaved as he had always behaved in class: keeping mostly to himself, but remaining ostensibly attentive and answering questions when called upon to speak, whispering the occasional remark to his classmates in hushed tones when he thought I was not looking. In fact, he behaved like most of the other boys in the class, or like any boy in any class that I have taught since. I needed urgently to believe that I had made some indelible and positive impact on Amir after our talk. I thought perhaps that Amir looked less withdrawn than before; I told myself that this was not something I was simply imagining. What I did not tell Amir was that I had a plan, a good surprise (I hoped) for Amir and his father, with positive results for the long-term future.

One evening I spoke to Christopher about what I planned to do, telling him about the whole episode of Amir's passionate confession, and then confessed my scheme. "I'm not sure it's the best way to go," he said over dinner, expressing his ambivalence. I sensed an argument coming but told myself to be patient. I knew I would be able to reason with Christopher. We were at the coffee shop downstairs from our flat. Because of our busy teaching jobs, neither of us had any time to cook at home. Luckily, Christopher and I did not have any children to feed. It was so much easier this way when the two of us could just have quick meals after work together. With children, life would have been so much more complicated; we would not have had the luxury to engage in meaningful conversations over dinner about anything and everything, about things that happened at work, or new revelations about teaching that we learnt in the course of our professional lives. There were no children to distract us from enriching each other's minds over the span of a meal. Both of us had agreed that the world was overcrowded enough without us producing offspring to feed on the earth's dwindling resources.

Besides, I had always taken for granted that our respective students were like our surrogate children anyway. We nurtured them, taught them, helped them to speak and write better and become better people, shaped them by leading them through our examples as caring educators. I am particularly proud when ex-schoolboys (the small handful who manage to find the time to do so) visit me years later to drop by my classes or the staff room to say hello, to show me how far they have arrived in life, and to hand me gifts of appreciation for my patience with them during their student days. Can any schoolteacher ask for anything more?

This is not to say that Christopher had not occasionally brought up the topic of having children, especially during the first few years of our marriage. "Don't you ever wish to have a baby in your arms? I do, sometimes."

"But Christopher, we've talked about this."

"Yes, I know..." Then an uncomfortable silence, with Christopher giving the impression that he was being forced to agree or accept my stance.

A similar silence ensued after I told him over dinner about Amir and what I hoped to do. He picked at his food, frowning, his expressive eyes now narrowed, his quietude expressing a private disapproval, even as he was also reluctant to disagree openly with me. "I know you don't approve, Christopher," I told him as he chewed on, not saying a word. "But I think you're wrong. I cannot just stand by and do nothing." I decided then to pick at my own plate of fried noodles with my chopsticks. The coffee shop was crowded as usual at this time of the evening, so I had to speak a bit louder to be heard. At another table next to ours, there was a young Chinese couple practically shouting at each other over the squeals and shrill laughter of a pair of restless toddlers between them.

Christopher, who was now drinking from a bowl of soup with a spoon, stayed silent. He knew better than to convince me when I had already made up my mind, although sometimes I wished he would be more antagonistic towards me. After a while, however, he did speak, choosing his words carefully: "You're a great teacher, sweetheart. I'm sure Amir was lucky to have spoken to you instead of some other teacher, who might have passed judgement on him, or asked him to stop being gay altogether, making him feel worse than what he must already be feeling."

"Actually, I'm not sure that I was the best person he could have spoken to. But now that he has spoken to me, I *have* to do something; I cannot possibly leave it alone. It'd be the absolutely wrong thing to do, leaving this matter alone!"

The couple with the noisy toddlers was now struggling to feed their children from messy dishes of rice and vegetables on the table, using fingers to insert bits of food into their children's mouths. I noticed this at the corner of my eye as Christopher replied: "Yes, I agree that something must be done. Your student, Amir, sounds like he's in a kind of rut. It must be hard growing up and learning that you are gay; it must be especially hard for a boy like him, being Muslim and all, and given his family situation, with a father who would certainly disapprove of his son's sexuality. Yes, I think you're right, dear. Something *must* be done. And I'm certain that you're the right person to help. You're Amir's teacher after all, and you obviously care a lot for your students. I'm sure you'll be able to handle this matter delicately, and I'm certain that something good will come out of this."

"That's right," I replied, smiling uncertainly at my husband. His words were encouraging, but there was still the start of a frown quivering across his gleaming forehead, marring his pale face ever so slightly. I always joked that Christopher looked more Northern Indian than Eurasian; he must have gotten his fair skin from his late mother, whose family originated from India, although the older he became, Christopher's late Portuguese father's baldness began to manifest through his receding hairline. That shadow of a frown threatened to age his handsome face further. "I'm really glad now that Amir *did* speak to me," I continued, hoping to straighten out my husband's frown. "And now that he's spoken to me, I believe it's my duty to help. I think my plan will work. I'm sure something good *will* come out of all this. You'll see, Christopher."

"After I consulted my husband about this," I tell my boys now, "he agreed that I had my student's best interests at heart, and supported me in what I planned to do."

What I do not tell the boys is how, that very night after dinner with Christopher, while I was lying in bed and he was snoring lightly beside me, I fantasised that Amir and I were walking on a beach in some distant future.

As the fantasy unfolded in my ever-active imagination, I wanted it to be a happy vision of an ideal future that could very well result from my actions. The setting could have been a beach on either the western or eastern coastline of the country, where families loved to visit with their picnic baskets over the weekend, flying kites, building sandcastles or wading into the waves, while in the distance container and cargo ships hovered like something left unsaid along that faint line between sea and sky.

Amir, in his mid-twenties, was walking beside me. I imagined that the sun was slowly setting to our right. A rugged sort of handsomeness was slowly emerging through his facial features, shyly but assuredly. He was going to make a lot of girls happy in the future.

Not girls, boys. I realised my mistake. How could I have forgotten what being gay meant?

As we walked together in my imagined scenario, I decided to ask this future version of Amir: "What are you doing now with your life? Are you happy, Amir? Has everything worked out for you in the end?"

"Yes, Mrs de Souza," he replied, calmly and confidently. "I just left university and I'm looking for a job now. I don't have a boyfriend, not yet anyway, but I'm dating somebody now and it looks promising."

"That's wonderful, Amir," I replied, smiling. "But remember, don't rush into anything. The worst thing you can do is to make irrational decisions that might end up blowing up in your face."

"I know, Mrs de Souza. I promise to think long and hard before I jump into anything. I wouldn't want to make a mistake and ruin my chances at happiness."

"Yes, that's good, Amir. We sometimes only get one chance at happiness in life."

"Just one?"

"Okay, I'm being melodramatic. But I mean it. Grab your happiness when you can see it. If you're certain that the person you have your eye on is the right one, never let him go. Or you might lose him for good and the rest of your life would be filled with regret." I cringed slightly at how sentimental I sounded. But this was my version of things to come; I wanted to be able to say such things to Amir, happy, sentimental things. I needed to know that Amir could be happy in my dream of his future.

"I know," Amir replied, serenely.

There was a pause, then Amir continued: "Also, I wanted to let you know that I have applied with the Ministry to become a teacher. I might not get the job, but I'm hoping to because, you know, I've always dreamed of becoming a teacher like you."

"Thank you so much, Amir. That's one of the nicest things any of my students has ever said to me. And if you need me to write you a letter of recommendation, please let me know. I'd gladly do it. You'd make a terrific teacher, Amir."

"No, thank *you*, Mrs de Souza." Amir stopped walking. "I want to be a teacher just like you, so that I can one day ruin my students' lives in the way that you have ruined mine—"

I gasped and woke up. I had dozed off without my knowledge. My waking dream had slipped into a real one. At which point in my fantasy about Amir had I even closed my eyes? Christopher shifted beside me but remained deeply and comfortably in his spacious world of slumber. I sat up in bed for a couple more minutes. After waiting for my heart to slow down, I finally settled into a supine position again. That last part was only a dream, I told myself, before closing my eyes, consciously this time. I struggled for about an hour before sinking back into unconsciousness.

CHAPTER 6

"I MUST ADMIT that I was nervous when picking up the phone to dial his home number," I confess to the boys in class.

I had retrieved Amir's telephone number from his school records and planned to make the call over the weekend. It was late Saturday morning and I knew that Amir would be on campus; he was a member of the school's Amateur Drama Society, which conducted regular rehearsals and acting workshops in the assembly hall every Saturday morning without fail. I made it a point to lean back in my favourite armchair in the living room as the ringing on the end of the line filled my ear. I felt like I was bracing myself for what was to come. This *is* the right thing to do, I reminded myself. I willed myself to feel optimistic. I was also gathering courage, in case the conversation turned ugly, in which case I would take the moral high ground and engage Amir's father in a battle of words and reason. I would insist that *both* of us keep in mind that Amir's happiness was at stake here.

A man picked up the phone after the third ring.

"Hello?" He had a low but resonant voice, and sounded as if he had been pulled away from another activity that had been preoccupying him.

"Hello? Is this Mr Yusuf?"

"Yes, who is this?" I thought Mr Yusuf sounded educated and articulate, but his tone was gruff and impatient.

"Sorry to disturb you, Mr Yusuf. This is Mrs de Souza. You haven't met me before. I'm Amir's English teacher from school."

"Yes?" Mr Yusuf sounded like he could not wait to get off the phone.

"Again, I'm really sorry to bother you on a Saturday morning. I was wondering if I could meet with you for us to have a friendly chat. It's regarding your son."

There was a long pause.

"Mr Yusuf, you still there?"

"Can we just talk about it over the phone? I...I might be travelling over the next few months and will have no time to meet anyone. Has Amir done something wrong? Have I forgotten to sign some form?"

"I think, Mr Yusuf, it might be better if we spoke in person. Would you be free any time today or next Saturday around this time?"

"Er, no, I won't be free. Is this very important? It's about Amir, right? Can we just talk about it over the phone now?"

I frowned as I cradled the phone against my ear. I really wanted to meet Amir's father in person, and as soon as possible, while I still possessed the courage to talk to him. I scanned the room around me, wondering where my husband could be at that instant. He had to be in the study, poring over his students' homework assignments. Even if he silently disapproved of this phone call, I still wished he was nearby, maybe sitting beside me on the sofa, supporting me through his presence alone.

"Well, Mr Yusuf. It's about a sensitive topic and I thought that perhaps a one-to-one would be more appropriate for what I wish to say."

Mr Yusuf paused a little longer this time before he replied, now even more grumpily: "I'm sorry, I *don't* have free time. Can you just tell me? We can talk on the phone. Just tell me what you want with Amir. He's not around. He's at school."

"I know that, Mr Yusuf. I just wanted to speak with you alone. I was hoping you'd understand that what I want to say is really very important, very sensitive, and it would be really good if we—"

"No," Amir's father rudely interrupted; he had not really raised his voice, yet it had sounded like a verbal attack. "I don't have time. Let's talk now."

I was getting flustered. I took a couple of quick, deep breaths. "All right, Mr Yusuf."

I was imagining a grouchy, skinny, old Malay man on the other end of the line, watching a television playing softly before him or reading the newspapers, trying his best to get the woman on the phone to say just what was on her mind, so that he could get back to whatever he had been doing.

"Mr Yusuf, like I said before, it's about your son, Amir. If you like, I guess...I guess we can talk over the phone. I'll try to keep this as brief as possible, so that I won't take up too much of your time."

Amir's father was keeping very quiet. He must have been thinking to himself: *Too late for that, isn't it.* I wondered what was playing on television in his home; although to be fair, I heard nothing playing in the background through the phone.

"I just have a few things to say," I continued, trying not to let irritation creep into my own voice. "Things regarding Amir which I think are very important that you should try to understand."

"I'm listening."

Are you really listening, Mr Yusuf? I thought.

"Thank you. You see, I don't know if Amir has told you anything—"

"No, nothing. Amir said nothing. Amir never says anything."

A sharp interruption again. At the same time, I thought it sounded like something with more meaning than Mr Yusuf intended to convey. Perhaps Amir's father was just being sarcastic, but he also sounded resentful about Amir's reluctance to share much of himself with his father.

I stopped myself from too much into his words, and charged politely on. "Okay, but Amir *has* said something to me. In fact, we had a long chat a couple of days ago. Amir spoke to me about many things regarding his private life, things I would like to share with you, because I think...I think it would help you to get to know your son better. It will help to improve your relationship with him, which is what he must want more than anything else in the world."

I was met with silence.

Taking another breath, I spoke on. "Your son, Amir, is a really brave boy, Mr Yusuf. He has been through a lot all on his own, with nobody to talk to. That's why, I think, he finally mustered the courage to approach me. I really applaud him for it. Your son is a remarkable boy, Mr Yusuf."

I paused. Why was Amir's father being so persistently quiet? There was not even a single encouraging grunt. I could have been speaking to a wall. But I had to assume that Mr Yusuf was still there. I needed him to be sympathetic, and to listen with an open heart and mind. I tried to imagine that Mr Yusuf was like my own father, a man who buried his face in the newspapers the few times that he was home, who ate the meals his wife cooked for him in silence, a silence nobody could penetrate because he would either snap at you if you did, or dismiss you quickly and ignore you more obviously than ever before. My mother had not stood for it and would ramble in front of him about how he was never around and about what a useless husband he was because he was always ignoring her; and he would carry on ignoring her, unperturbed, thus pushing her further into a familiar state of hysterical rage.

"Amir is a growing boy," I was saying into the phone. "Soon he will become a man and he will have to make important decisions for himself." As I was speaking, I realised that I was starting to sound condescending. I had to find better words!

"And as we both know, it's hard growing up with nobody to talk to at this age, especially when one learns that one is different from the other boys around him." I was rambling. I was nervous.

"Different?" At last, a response. I was relieved. Perhaps Amir's father was starting to show *some* interest in his son.

"Yes, Mr Yusuf, your son is...is, yes, *very* different."

Why was I repeating such a banal euphemism? What in the world did 'different' mean? I did not intend to sound as if Amir was deformed or morally corrupt. I was describing neither a freak nor a criminal.

"What I mean to say is...your son is *gay*, Mr Yusuf. Your son's having difficulty coming to terms with the fact, this undeniable fact, about being homosexual."

The silence was deafening this time. I could not even hear Amir's father breathing on the other end. I rambled on: "I know this must come as a shock to you, Mr Yusuf. But I told him, and I would like to let you know too, that I thought it was admirable how he has been able to own up to this aspect of himself, that he was able to speak to me about this matter. You see, Mr Yusuf, although we both know it can be difficult being homosexual, especially in this country..."

I noted that words like 'gay' and 'homosexual' were echoing like deep explosions in my mind every time I said these words, as if I was pronouncing offensive curse words. I wondered if these silent explosions were taking place too in Mr Yusuf's mind, each time I uttered them again.

"...although it can be hard to be gay in our present society, I believe—I really believe—that our country is changing by leaps and bounds every day. And one day, gays *will* be accepted into the fabric of society. It will be perfectly normal to be homosexual, one day; I'm sure you can see my point of view, can't you, Mr Yusuf?"

I waited for him to respond.

Finally, he did: "You're talking rubbish."

It was said so curtly, so coldly and resolutely that, at first, I was not sure that I had heard him correctly. Mr Yusuf's words struck me like a blow to the head.

I hurriedly recovered. "Excuse me, I think you've misunderstood my intentions. I don't believe that there is anything *wrong* with being homosexual. I don't think Amir has any choice in the matter. I think that, as a reasonable man, you'd agree with me. I don't think whether it's wrong or right is what this conversation is about. And I'm sure you can agree, at this moment in his young adult life, Amir must be going through a hard time coming to terms with this important part of himself—"

"You're talking rubbish," Mr Yusuf said again, his voice even sharper. His gravelly voice was still low but raised a slight pitch higher and louder. It was a concise verbal attack. He was on the brink of losing his temper, but he was also doing all he could to keep his voice in check. Something in his voice also possessed a deadening quality.

I envisioned Amir's father grabbing the phone tighter in his hand, a frown deepening on his wrinkled forehead, his heart beating faster, in the same way that my own heart was beating faster in my chest now. I knew that since I was the one who had started this conversation, I had no choice but to finish it. "Listen, Mr Yusuf, if you love your son, you'll *listen* to what I'm saying to you. Your son's in an extremely unfortunate time of his life right now, and he needs his father, his only parent left in this world, to be there for him, to guide and support him especially through this time in his life. I'm sure that as his concerned and loving father, you'd not find it hard to agree that it is Amir's state of mind that is of utmost importance here."

I was starting to sound like a caricature of a placating civil servant. "When he spoke to me, I could tell that he was in a state of internal crisis and turmoil and that he needs someone like you, his father, to be there to tell him everything will turn out fine; that being gay is only ever just a small aspect of one's life. Amir has a long and meaningful and happy life ahead of him, wouldn't you agree, Mr Yusuf?"

Mr Yusuf still had not said another word. What a stubborn, unpleasant man!

"I think that right now, Amir must feel that he's caught in a rut; I think he feels trapped in his own skin and more than ever, he needs the people he loves to help him deal with these terrible feelings. I know that at the end of the day, you're probably a conservative man, Mr Yusuf, but I'm certain you can see the truth of what I'm saying to you right now. You must love your son very much. So if you love your son, you must realise that being gay is really, really far from being the end of the world. It is not as if your son is a murderer or a thief. Who anyone desires or falls in love with is surely none of anybody's business, Mr Yusuf. I'm sure you *must* agree with me. The one important thing for you to think about now is Amir's happiness, Mr Yusuf. You must be there for him. Your son needs you more than ever, before these difficult feelings of confusion and sadness consume him and transform him into an unhappy adult. Are you still there, Mr Yusuf? Do you understand what I'm trying to tell you?"

As I recount to my classroom of boys an abridged but still emotionally wrought (I am hoping) version of what I said to Amir's father, I become aware that perhaps the remembered version of my speech over the phone is overly long and dramatic, with added emphases that were not there before. For example, I am not sure now if I had actually included that statement about how it was none of anybody's business whom a person chooses to fall in love with. I must have thrown that in for theatrical effect and added poignancy. Perhaps I had merely caught sight of one of the birthday-cum-farewell cards given to me by my students. A trite sentence like "We'll love and remember you" (not personally handwritten but printed as part of the original card), coupled with the visual mess of flowers strewn on my table, might have had an effect on my brain and on my recollection of the past.

I then remember that my hour with my boys is almost up. I have been telling them a watered down version of the phone conversation, picking only choice sentences from memory to indicate feelings of frustration or outrage, careful not to allude explicitly to Amir's sexuality in my retelling. Yet I have still managed to carry on for too long. I will have to round up everything that I have been meaning, or not meaning, to say. I must finish this story.

All this while, Mr Yusuf had said nothing on the phone, and so when I completed my speech, I decided to wait for Amir's father to come through with an appropriate response. I was inclined to just hold the phone in my hand, letting him take all the time he needed to say something that would show that he had heard every word. He had to understand that whatever he chose to say or do from this moment on had to derive from the fact that he was Amir's father; that he loved his son, as all fathers must love their children.

What happened next instead was worse than any verbal

outburst that I had anticipated. After several long silent moments, Amir's father firmly put his phone back in its cradle with a gentle click. The line went dead.

CHAPTER 7

"AFTER THE WEEKEND had passed, I went back to school, still remembering the mostly one-sided conversation I'd had with my student's father who rudely hung up on me. I even discussed the conversation with my husband."

To Christopher's credit, he never once told me I never should have called Amir's father in the first place. He just nodded, trying to repress his silent disapproval. What was done was done; at least both of us agreed wholeheartedly on this. Over brunch on Sunday at our favourite coffee shop downstairs, after seeing my despondent look, Christopher offered some encouraging words: "I think you said all you could say to the man. I'm sure you were reasonable, and your words must have made a positive impact on Amir's father, who probably *is* an introverted and conservative man, and who is now also terribly confused. I think whether he likes it or not, he's been forced to think long and hard about everything you've said about his one and only son."

I had an afternoon lesson with Amir's class the coming Monday. I was worried about how Amir would feel or react when he finally saw me. Would Mr Yusuf have confronted him about the phone call? Would Amir be too embarrassed or hurt to look his teacher in the eye?

I was not too surprised when I entered the classroom on Monday and saw that Amir's usual seat by the window was conspicuously empty.

"Does anyone know where Amir is?" I asked the rest of the boys. Someone told me that he had not come to school at all, since he had not seen Amir in any of the other classes that they usually attended together in the earlier part of the morning. Another boy also said that he had not seen Amir during morning assembly.

For the rest of the day, I taught my classes in my usual no-nonsense style, but a part of my mind remained entrenched in worry and doubt about whether I had done the right thing in calling Mr Yusuf. I wondered if Amir had perhaps been grounded by his father, or if his father now had an unshakeable distrust for the school or specifically for me. Maybe he was planning to take Amir out of the school for good, and transfer him to another institution.

Christopher had been the only other soul I confided in regarding the phone call. I told nobody else in the school. I certainly had no plans to tell the principal, for fear that Mr Ong might reprimand me for being 'unprofessional' and for interfering in the private affairs of students. I recalled that Mr Ong had actually met Yusuf's father when the latter came to thank him for allowing Amir to be promoted despite the boy's unimpressive marks. I partly hoped that maybe the principal would commiserate with me and tell me he was not surprised by Mr Yusuf's reaction, since Amir's father had seemed like one of those typically well-meaning but small-minded parents whose hands he had shaken over the years. In the end, I just kept the conversation with Mr Yusuf to myself.

I wondered if I should make another phone call, this time from the staff room when everyone else was out at the canteen for lunch. Maybe I would ask for Amir this time; or if Amir's father picked up the phone again, I would ask *him* about why Amir had not come to school. Eventually I decided that I would wait it out, and told myself I would not think about it again until Amir came back to school. Once Amir was back in class, I would ask to see him just for a few minutes and request that he tell me if anything new had happened at home, just to gauge if my conversation with Mr Yusuf had made a positive or negative impact.

Most of all, I needed desperately to know if I had done the right thing. I still had high hopes that I must have planted a seed of much needed self-reflection in Mr Yusuf's stubborn mind, and that the effect of our tense conversation would bear fruit later when Amir and his father bonded better as parent and child. And from such a strong, loving relationship with his father, Amir would then be able to come confidently into his own as a mature adult, at last, with unshakeable self-esteem.

CHAPTER 8

I DO NOT tell my boys about a terrible nightmare (not a waking fantasy, this time, but a real dream) I had at the end of the same day when Amir did not show up for class. It was a frightful dream that I still recall to this day. And if I relate it now in the midst of my story about Amir, I might make it more frightening than when it first occurred in my sleep. I need to finish talking about Amir, even as the nightmare overtakes my mind without warning.

This dream featured neither Amir nor my mother. I was standing at the front of a classroom, quite likely the same one I am in now. It was a familiar scene, except none of the boys had any faces; or their faces were so blurred or washed out in my dream that I could not make them out. Each of the boys raised his hand to ask me a question. When I gestured at each faceless boy to speak, his voice would sound remarkably like Amir's.

One boy asked: "Did your mother love you, Mrs de Souza?"

He had no mouth, but I heard the question loud and clear. Before I answered, I wanted to gaze out the window to see if the school field would be there as it always was, hoping the familiar sight would distract me from the faceless heads beaming at me like coins of glowing, featureless flesh.

Outside the window, there was no field; there were only clouds, as if I was staring out an airplane window. I turned to the boy who had asked the question. "Yes," I answered, but was unable to bring forth the boy's name; without a face, the boy had no name. "Yes, I'm certain that in her own way, my mother loved me. I never questioned her love. She gave up a lot to love me. I cannot believe she did this because she felt she had no choice, or that she did it to please my father. She loved me in spite of her complaining and nagging. I'm sure of it."

Another boy raised his hand. "And what about your father? Did he love you?"

"No, I don't think he did." I was shocked by my answer, and by my lucidity in this frightening dream. "He might have loved me once, maybe when I was a newborn. But I think he eventually stopped loving me after he stopped loving his wife, which is why my mother slowly learned to hate him, and maybe why Mother later learnt to hate me too."

A boy at the back of the class raised his hand. "Did you kill your mother?"

"No, I didn't. She died of a heart attack while doing laundry. I found her lying on the floor in the kitchen with clothes draped over her face, her curly hair sticking out messily from under a fallen blouse. I was already living with Christopher at the time, and she was living on her own in the year since Father had passed away. I came home over the weekend to visit, and found her on the floor like that. It was a fitting way to die, I thought cruelly at the time. She died like how she lived, blinded by her anger at her husband and at the world for not allowing her to be free, for not allowing her to live her own dreams and discover a better life."

Another boy raised his hand. "Did you kill your father?"

"No. He died of liver failure while in India visiting friends and relatives. He drank a lot, although he was never drunk when he was home with Mum and me. His body was cremated in India and the urn containing his ashes was shipped to us. But I was not unhappy that he had died. Although I wished that after his death, and after I moved out to live with Christopher, my mother would start a life of her own. Instead, she stayed at home all day, surviving on the money that I dutifully transferred into her bank account every month. She never used the money I gave her to make anything new of her life. She only cooked and cleaned and spent hours looking out the window feeling sorry for herself. She never went out, except to buy groceries. She never called anyone on the phone and she hardly ever watched television. She just spent hours by the kitchen window, leaning out and staring. Maybe she had loved my father after all, and keeping herself at home helped to remind her of him."

"Did you kill your husband?" another boy asked. This boy was sitting where Amir would have sat in real life. It was Amir's voice issuing from the mouthless countenance, but I could not be certain that it was actually him.

"No, I did not. He died of cancer. Although in the last few weeks, I did wish, against my will and my love for him, that he would die quickly, so his pain would stop."

"Did you kill yourself?" It was the same boy who had asked the last question. I am almost certain now that it must have been Amir who had spoken.

"Why? Am I dead? Is this why I am here? Because I have killed myself? Is this some kind of afterlife, some version of purgatory? Maybe I did kill myself. Maybe I killed myself by not having any children to look after. Maybe I killed myself by ending my family's bloodline. Maybe I killed myself by being a teacher when I could have been a writer, an actress, a pianist, a travelling musician, even a flight attendant. I ended all of these dreams by being a teacher straight away after school was over. The people at the Ministry said during the interview that they liked my enthusiasm and my passion, as if they had really known my enthusiasm and passion. I have always known how to put on a show, like how I pretended I loved my father when I was young while he was busy ignoring my mother, like how I pretended to care about my mother when she was left alone to fend for herself. Maybe I've been dead for a long time, even when I was alive. Is that what you're telling me? Is that what you're all trying to say?"

Then one by one, all the boys' hands began rapidly to shoot up. I nodded at the sea of faceless students, signalling them to speak. And they said all at once, chanting hypnotically in unison and repeating the question until I woke up with a start: "Did you kill Amir? Did you kill Amir? Did you kill Amir? Did you kill Amir? Did you kill Amir…"

CHAPTER 9

I CARRY ON quickly with my story. "It was Mr Ong who broke the news the moment I stepped into the staff room on Wednesday morning. Many of the other teachers were also there and had not yet left for morning assembly, since the head of assembly was hovering in front of my desk."

Mr Ong had wanted to break the news to me himself. His sleeves were folded all the way up to his elbows. Students made fun of him because of the halting manner with which he tended to make announcements over the intercom, and for the measured but plodding way he liked to pace the school corridors. Mr Ong was standing at my table with a hand on his waist and the other hand holding up his chin. He looked comical, like he was trying to solve a maths equation in his head. Then he lowered his hand from his chin and cleared his throat politely.

"Rose, I'm afraid I have some bad news," he said. "It's about your student from Class 2E6: Amir. I'm afraid…I'm afraid he has died."

I felt something at the back of my mind bottom out.

"…and the funeral's this evening," Mr Ong was saying. "But I've been informed by Amir's father that nobody in the school should come. I called him personally and that was all he had to say. The funeral is for family members only."

Had I missed something? Had Mr Ong said something about the cause of death? "H-how did it happen?"

"I'm afraid it was...suicide," Mr Ong replied, this time lowering his head, placing his arms solemnly behind his back. "If you want to, you can read it in the papers this morning. I'm going to make a small announcement this morning at the assembly. I think I will have to say something appropriate... many of his classmates will have known by now...they'll be upset, I suspect. I know you must be affected too. You are, *were*, after all, his form teacher, also his English teacher. We're all very upset by this. I left a copy of the newspaper on your table if you'd like to keep the article about him. A reporter called me and asked some questions. I know you'd have been a better person to answer those questions but I thought I'd just answer them for you. I didn't want the reporter to bother you. The questions were rather intrusive and for Amir's sake and for our school's reputation, I didn't want the reporter to write too much about this. I don't want the press casting us in any bad light. I'm sure you understand. Also, because of my many meetings with parents, I couldn't find the time yesterday afternoon to tell you about the reporter calling and breaking the news about Amir. I'm really sorry, Rose. I hope we'll be able to put this tragedy behind us...now, I think I have to go take care of assembly. You don't have to attend if you don't want to. If there's anything important, I'll be sure to inform you. And if you'd like to speak to me about this later, feel free to find me, or make an appointment with my secretary. Okay... all right then..."

Mr Ong hesitated, rather awkwardly, not sure if he had said everything he needed to, before he quietly withdrew from the staff room, along with the other teachers, some of whom politely whispered their condolences to me on their way out. "I'm so sorry, Rose. Such awful news," somebody said as he walked past, though I could not tell who it was. Such words made it sound like it had been my own son who had passed away. I found this funny for some reason, but did not smile.

When the staff room was finally empty, I sat down at my table. Mr Ong had indeed placed a folded newspaper (turned to the relevant page) on my desk. Amir had not even made it to the front page. The news about his death was buried in between an article about the rising tax rates in the coming year and a larger article about an illegal strike conducted by some foreign workers. There was not even a photograph of Amir to accompany the report. Instead there was a chart printed at the bottom of a page that recorded the hike in the number of teen suicides over the last five years. I picked up the paper and brought the article closer to my face, afraid I might miss something:

A fourteen-year-old Malay student, Amir Hussein bin Yusuf, jumped to his death on late Sunday night from his twelfth floor window. His body was discovered by neighbours on the ground floor the following morning. He was pronounced dead by paramedics, who confirmed that he had died immediately upon impact.

The police have confirmed that there is no suspicion of foul play.

This is another case in a growing trend of teen suicides

that have been occurring with alarming frequency. So far this year, there have been a total of twenty-two teen suicides reported, a significant increase from last year when only ten were reported (see chart on right).

Some experts have previously suggested that the rising stress levels of students, and academic pressures to succeed in school, play a huge part in this disturbing development.

Amir lived with his father and grandmother.

Principal Ong Lian Beng had little to say about Amir's behaviour in his school that could have provided a hint about why Amir chose to end his life. The boy had shown no outward signs of depression and was considered a less-than-average student in his cohort. He was also active in his school's drama club and was generally well-liked by peers.

His father and grandmother have declined to be interviewed.

Funeral arrangements have been made for this evening at...

I dropped the newspaper back on the table. The article said nothing, revealed absolutely nothing. If the reporter had found a way to speak to me, I would have probably said nothing too. Would it have helped if I had told the reporter what Amir had confessed to me? How would his family have taken the extraneous 'bad' news about who Amir had been when he was alive? What would that have done for Amir's reputation?

Did one's reputation really matter after death?

And Mr Ong was right about having the school's prestige to consider. A suicide could have a negative impact on how the public perceived the institution.

And would I also have told the reporter that it was me, Mrs de Souza, Amir's form and English teacher, who had caused Amir's death? I was the one who had forced Amir and his father into a direct confrontation with each other, forcing Amir to retreat into his bedroom, compelling him to push open a window...

I heard Mr Ong speaking distantly outside on the microphone, making his morning announcements to a school hall full of inattentive boys. What were those boys thinking now that Amir was gone? Did the ones whom Amir had crushes on even suspect that Amir was gay, let alone suspect that he might have been attracted to them? Those boys must have never known sadness in the way Amir had known sadness, loneliness, bitterness—and all before turning sixteen. What would they think if they knew about Amir's secret fantasies? Would they hate him? Would they still make fun of him; would they dare to make fun of the dead? I would not put it past them.

Would they, in time, forget Amir altogether? Was I the only person in this school who gave a damn about Amir then? Was there *anyone* who cared at all about poor Amir? He had said, after all, that he had told nobody his secret. He had trusted *me*, his teacher, and only me.

A tear slipped down my right cheek. Was I filled with regret and remorse over what I had done? Was I crying because I had actually cared for Amir? Or was I merely feeling sorry for myself? If that was the case, surely I had no right to cry. No right at all. I wiped a hand across my face, then pressed it against the guilty eye, making sure no more tears fell.

Amir's face kept appearing in my mind. I imagined Mr Yusuf's face too, although I had never met him in person. What could have happened to have made Amir climb out his window? Had father and son fought? Had his father brought up the fact that a teacher had called their home, telling him that his son was gay, and henceforth did Amir transform instantaneously into a cruel disappointment to his father; his father who was a hardworking, religious man and who had ultimately wasted his life taking care of a homosexual son? Did Amir stand up to his father, telling him that he did not care if being gay was against their religion, that his father had to accept who he was, or else? And what would Mr. Yusuf have said, in response? Probably something horrible and mean like a cup of acid flung at a face. Did Mr. Yusuf threaten to disown his son if Amir did not promise to 'change' and become 'a real man'? And where had Amir's grandmother been in all this? Had she been sitting in a corner of the living room, throwing herself into the latest soap opera on television, or hiding in the kitchen, telling herself that such fights always resolved themselves in the end; that Amir was a good boy and would listen to his father and do what he was told; that all it would take was a little bit of shouting and scolding and a whole lot of discipline to wake Amir up from delusions about being gay?

My body was trembling. I was holding up my head with both hands now. No, I refused to think about this. I refused to dwell upon this. I had a whole day of school ahead. My students would expect me to be calm, poised and composed, as I had always been. I had always prided myself on never losing my cool at work; I was not about to start now.

CHAPTER 10

I TELL THE boys in my classroom: "Although I was saddened and traumatised, I forced myself to move on with the rest of my day..." I do not say that as the day had worn on, I dearly missed my tall, burly, balding, paunchy husband. During the mid-day break that morning, I had at least twenty-five minutes of quiet and solitude in my classroom, with all the boys out at the canteen or playing soccer on the school field outside. I do not tell my boys that after having absorbed the news of Amir's suicide, I closed my eyes and listened to the fan spinning in the staff room somewhere above me, similar to the fan that is spinning above the boys I am addressing now. I knew Christopher would probably have been busy running around in his own school at that point in the day, so it would have been useless to try and call him, just to hear his voice.

Amir's classmates tried to behave as if nothing had happened. Amir's seat was conspicuously empty, yet no one said anything. All my students that day pretended that Amir had simply...vanished. Perhaps they whispered about it amongst themselves after class or during break times. As for me, I had no one to talk to about it. I wished Christopher was there.

I'd first met Christopher during one of our classes

together at the local university. It was a sociology lesson, an intimate tutorial setting with a head lecturer. There were only about seven students in the room. The faces of the other students are a blur to me now. I only remember Christopher, a slimmer man then, with his full head of semi-curly hair that had been neatly and fastidiously cropped at the sides, his bright, brown eyes and lopsided grin. I cannot recall what he had been wearing that day. His voice had been the same as it was all throughout our marriage, smooth and warm, when he spoke during tutorials. It was only by chance that we were placed in the same module together, as he was from the sciences while I was in the humanities; he had opted to take sociology as a cross-faculty elective. And he would not have asked me out on a date were we not in the same course, which, in those days, meant having lunch together in a quieter corner of the school canteen, or studying at the reference section of the university library.

Then one day my head fell to rest on his shoulder. I cannot recall where this had taken place exactly, but I know it had happened as naturally as falling rain in the middle of a sunny afternoon in this country's humid, tropical climate. It could have taken place while we were discussing dreams of becoming teachers in the future, what kind of teachers we would become, what subjects we would teach, which schools and what kind of students we would encounter. We were still young, but back then we had not felt young at all. We felt as if the rest of our lives were already taking place and that since we had found each other, that somehow every day would stay the same from then on. Every new experience or future challenge would form but a small and manageable part of the luminous backdrop of our lives together as a couple. There was a certain invincibility that came with being in love. Our relationship meant that we could be braver, more daring, more outspoken about our views, especially after we finally became certified as teachers and were assigned to our respective schools. After we got married, Christopher would come back home and regale me with stories about things he had said to his students. He would boast about how attentive his students became when they learned that he was 'not like all the other boring teachers'. He probably had an over-inflated idea of himself as a teacher at the time, but I loved him and chose to believe what he told me.

Christopher was not a disciplinarian in his early years as a teacher. According to him, he had been quick to crack jokes in class and eager to make his students feel as if they could say anything in the classroom. He wanted mathematics to be fun, not like the way other subjects, particularly physics and chemistry, were commonly taught. He wanted students to understand the relevance of mathematics in their daily lives; and beyond his subject matter, he would pepper his lessons with statements about how materialistic he felt the country was becoming, how education served no purpose other than to help students find menial jobs in a nation driven by the appearance of global relevance and economic success, how multiculturalism in this country was more about grudging tolerance than sincere and warm-hearted cohesiveness, how this little island was moving so far ahead of itself that it was forgetting the roots of its cultural heritages and diverse histories, and all this while scrawling formulae about differentiating equations and uncovering the secrets behind complex trigonometric functions on his classroom blackboard.

All this changed when a few students, as well as some teachers, complained about him to the school principal. He never found out who they were, as the complaints were submitted anonymously, but he was warned by the principal not to stray too far from academic discussions; and even within the realm of academics, he had to 'keep to the script' (how Christopher had put it, one evening after he asked if maybe teaching was not the right profession for him, after all) or else his teaching contract would not be renewed by the end of the year.

Christopher's transformation had not been immediate. In the weeks that followed, Christopher told me that something was slowly snapping apart within him. It was not anything dramatic. His students slowly realised that he was speaking less and less in class, frowning more, and soon he was also no longer cracking jokes. Their mathematics teacher was withdrawing into himself; or to put it another way, one version of Christopher was fading away, while another was coming in to take its place. After enough time had lapsed, students and colleagues remarked on how fierce and grumpy Christopher had become. He told me that he became known as a silent but effective disciplinarian, much to the patronising approval of the school principal.

"This doesn't mean that I've given up," Christopher reminded me. "Even as I scold and make long, fearsome faces in class, I still manage to sneak in some surprising comment that my students don't expect. I tell them to 'wake up' and to 'stop being a nobody in life' and 'don't trust what anybody says, including me'. They're always surprised when they hear me say such things. They tend to expect me to reprimand them or give them a warning or threaten them with expulsion. When there's a will, there's a way. Creativity is the key in being a rebel within a repressive environment. And I *must* have my way in showing my students how to think for themselves in this bloody useless education system."

I could tell Christopher was still frustrated by how much he had to repress himself at school. But I was glad that at least he did not lose too much of his passion for teaching, and that he had found a way to insert his personality and his views into his classes. I wished that I possessed the fire that Christopher held inside him, the fire that he kept mostly hidden from everyone in his school, but which kept him going as a teacher still determined to make his mark on the world.

As a teacher, my own career had been, in my estimation, smooth sailing. From the start, I had hardly ever crossed any invisible lines of decorum. I maintained a cool, collected, yet friendly demeanour in the classroom and in front of fellow teachers. In this way, everyone found me 'safe' and 'predictable', 'a stern lady' and 'that classy teacher with big hair', labels that I wore with pride from the moment I entered St Nicholas Boys' School. As an English teacher, there was a reasonable amount of room in my lessons in which I could subtly invite ideas of subversion and alternative viewpoints from students, points of view that they normally would not express in other classes, in public or at home. I liked to think that this sense of 'rebelliousness' in me had been inspired by Christopher's example.

After years of teaching, I still consider the creative writing exercises that I conducted as the most rewarding part of my lessons. The exercises were supervised and marked by me alone, and students were encouraged to write about anything they wanted. Many students used this opportunity to write stories about murder and death and the supernatural, thinking that they would get a thrill out of 'shocking' their conservative-looking English teacher. But I always just marked them for their grammar and spelling and wrote finely legible comments on their scripts about how certain sentences could have been better composed.

"I love that my students find the exercise so liberating," I once told my husband. "My boys write all kinds of things; they can get pretty gory in their creative prose sometimes, especially when they write about ghosts and vampires and monsters in cellars and all that. But some also write stories that criticise the government or the school or their friends; some even reveal personal information about their families. I think the exercise might be cathartic for them. I mean, where else can they say or write about these things, right? And I *know* they sense my approval every time they think they've written something daring or outrageous, especially when I only ever make comments in class about how 'funny' and 'entertaining' their stories can be. I can tell they're grateful for the freedom that I've granted them during such exercises."

I might have been a 'safe' teacher, but I was glad that I always found the opportunity to make a truly valuable difference in my boys' lives. Although I must admit that over time, I might have become more irritable and prone to coldness and sarcasm in my later years, due to age and my dwindling patience for tardiness and stupidity. I like to think I still kept trying to be a good teacher; my fundamental intentions have stayed the same in wanting to make my students think for themselves.

As I thought about these creative writing exercises, I tried to think back on whether I could recall anything that Amir had written in such exercises. The problem was that I always made sure to return the guilty manuscripts back to their authors, not just so that they would read the comments that I had written on them, but also that the students could keep what they had written as poignant and haunting reminders of their hidden voices, voices that they had been conditioned to suppress. If I did not return the papers, it was usually because the students were absent on certain days, forcing me to keep their scripts indefinitely.

As I sat in my empty classroom, waiting for boys to stumble back in from their recess, gazing occasionally at Amir's empty seat, I vaguely remembered reading Amir's compositions and stories. I also recalled that nothing he had ever written had been remotely subversive or controversial. There was one time when he had written about how his father had taken him fishing. The expedition was described in only a few hundred words, and he had described his father as a smiling man who was exceedingly proud to see his own son wield a fishing rod and hook. He wrote that they had caught no fish one Sunday afternoon, but Amir had thoroughly enjoyed spending that time alone with his father. Although Amir had used simple words and short sentences in his story, he had impeccable grammar and spelling, unlike some of the other students who liked to use bombastic words to show off while stumbling clumsily through the misuse of tenses and the misspelling of even the simplest verbs and nouns.

As recess was drawing to a close, the school bell about to ring in a few minutes, I conjured up the narrative scene of Amir and his father in my head, inspired by what Amir must have written in his composition: the hot sun in the sky, a few clouds scudding overhead, the open sea—or was it a lake or a river, I was not quite sure—and his father (an older man with wispy, greying hair, as how I chose to imagine him, since I had never seen him) who would be holding Amir's hand, teaching him how to swing the line in a clear arc right over the water. There must have been other people in the scene, on the beach or along the harbour, watching a father and son as they waited for fish to bite. *How touching*, they must have thought.

I wanted very much to focus my inner eye on Amir's face as he turned to look up at his father, his father then turning to look down at his son, the sun in Amir's eyes, illuminating nothing but affection and serenity. Almost instantly, I could feel a tidal wave of hopelessness and grief rising up within me, feelings that I had been trying to repress all that morning. At the same time, Amir's empty chair loomed large before my literal vision from across the classroom. Questions banged on the lid of my mind: *What have you done? What kind of teacher do you think you are, messing with other people's lives? What have you done to his father and his poor grandmother? How dare you call yourself a teacher? How can you ever teach again? Why should any of your gullible students trust you, believe you, listen to you, learn from you, respect you?* I did all I could to push the wave of emotions back down. Now was not the time for self-beratement and self-pity.

I returned to the same scene, now slowly dissolving around the edges inside my imagination: Amir and his father were looking out at the horizon—or was it only the trees on the other side of a narrow river—both at the same time, their heads turning away from each other in slow motion. A few clouds crawled to a standstill. If there were birds in the sky, they suspended themselves now in mid-air and pinned themselves against the brightness. The water stopped stirring too, its resident fishes shuddering to a halt under the clear but immovable surface.

Amir was holding the fishing rod and he was smiling and the afternoon sunlight was brightening and closing in with such tenderness all around him, cradling him, keeping him in place, rendering him into something permanent, the glowing image of a boy sitting proudly beside his father now burnt into a page of memory for all time.

Then the bell sounded. Break time was over.

CHAPTER 11

IN ANOTHER DREAM (which, again, I do not reveal to the boys, but which haunts me now of all times while I am telling my story), I was sitting up in bed, but I knew that I was really asleep. I turned to see if Christopher was beside me, but his side of the bed was empty. Was his absence a premonition of some kind? Even in my dream, I was being reminded that Christopher was dying; the dream did not rescue me from the reality of Christopher lying in the hospital, waiting for me to come back and visit him; he was waiting for me even though he had insisted that I go home and take a shower and sleep in the comfort of our own bed, instead of resting on an uncomfortable couch beside his hospital bed.

In this dream, I was alone in my room. I got out of bed and went to the window. It was night, but there were no stars, no moon. Just the dark. There was a knock on my bedroom door. Oddly, I was unafraid. I went to the door and opened it. There was nobody there. So I walked out into the living room, or a room that looked like my living room. As this was a dream, everything was too hazy to be certain. All the hall lights seemed to be on. Amir was sitting in the same armchair where I had called his father more than a decade earlier. That terrible mistake.

This was not a horror movie, so there was no blood on Amir's face when he looked at me as I walked, or floated, towards him. He looked the same as when I had first known him: young, fresh and smiling. It felt strange to be dreaming about Amir after all that time. He was smiling, but not evilly, threateningly or bitterly. Then his face blurred and I could no longer figure out what he looked like any more, not exactly. Amir's whole figure shivered and was gone. The armchair was empty again.

CHAPTER 12

CHRISTOPHER'S TWO YOUNGER sisters, Theresa and Cynthia, and his colleagues from school all came to his funeral. It was a church funeral, as that was what he had asked for, so as to please his sisters, who were Christian. Hymns were sung and prayers said. I sat in the front pew but refused to join in. His sisters sitting beside me must have thought I was grieving silently, but I just did not want to sing or pray about things I did not believe in. Christopher would have approved of my rebelliousness.

That night in bed, I dreamt that I was back in the same church, with the same open coffin, except there was no one in the church with me, and the coffin was empty. Then I saw the back of somebody in the front pew, where I had sat during the funeral proceedings with his sympathetic siblings. I walked quickly to sit beside this person in my dream. He turned to me and I saw that it was Christopher himself: my sweet, handsome husband, his bald head gleaming from the light that drifted down from the church's high ceiling. Still paunchy, I realised; no longer emaciated from his illness.

"You looked good at the funeral," he was saying to me.

"You didn't look so good yourself," I replied. I wanted to cry but I was unable to.

"I hope you weren't too sad," he said, smiling, then reached over to hold my hand. I wanted to fight with him at this moment, to accuse him of leaving me alone. I wanted us to fight like we used to at the hospital, about matters concerning money or life support; the fighting made me feel as if he was still full of strength and that he would never leave me.

I held his hand. We were not going to fight. Both of us looked together at the empty coffin at the front of the church. "What do we do now?" I asked.

"We can just talk. It's a dream, so we have all the time in the world."

"We do?"

"Yes, we do. What do you want to talk about?"

"Are you happy?" I asked. "Are you in pain?"

"No, no pain. And yes, I'm happy; as happy as I can be without you, I suppose."

"I miss you, especially after the funeral, after I went back home…"

"I know. I was at home waiting for you. I'm always waiting for you; I'm sure you know that by now."

"Yes, I guess I do. But are you really happy? Were you happy when you were with me, when you were alive?"

"I was, Rose. I was very happy."

"Did you ever still wish, for example, that we had, well…"

"A child of our own?"

"Yes."

"I don't know. Sometimes I did wish we would become parents. Most times I didn't. I mean, we had made our bed and had to lie in it, right? We agreed from the start: no children."

"Yes, but did you ever want, I mean really want, to have a child? I know that I was the one who insisted."

"I won't deny that there were times I thought a child would add something to our lives. Imagine it: a version of you and me in a single baby, climbing up and down our furniture, swinging from our arms, calling us Mummy and Daddy."

"I'm sorry that I pressured you."

"What are you talking about? It was a mutual decision."

"When was the last time you wished you had a child?"

"There was only this one time at the hospital, when I just thought about how nice it would have been if we had a son or daughter to take care of you after I was gone."

"Would that be a good reason to have a child, Christopher? Just so the child could take care of me when I'm old and helpless?"

"No, I guess not. Look, Rose, I need to tell you something."

"Yes, honey?"

"You haven't called me that in a long time."

"Are we too old to be using such childish names on each other?"

"I still like it though."

"I'm happy that you do, honey."

"But seriously, I need to tell you something."

"Yes?"

"I really want you to be happy for me," he said.

"Is that it? I thought you were going to tell me the upcoming lottery results or something *important* like that. I could really use the money, you know, to buy a piano, a new oven..."

"Very funny, Rose."

"I thought you might think so."

"But seriously, I need you to listen. I want you to be happy—and to be healthy. Don't be like me: take plenty of antioxidants or something. Exercise, never touch a drop of alcohol."

"How funny—a ghost that nags."

"And do everything that you meant to do with me. You can always imagine that I'm there with you, all the time. Imagine that; it'd be like buying one ticket for two people. Think of the cost savings for all your trips from now on."

"A funny ghost that nags."

"You have the money that I left for you. Please use it. See the world. Go to Tibet, climb a mountain, visit an ashram, watch a concert in Vienna, catch an opera in Prague, a play in London. Just retire early, and do...everything, sweetheart. Everything that you could possibly do without injuring yourself."

"I thought maybe I would like to write a book, maybe a romance or a thriller, in my free time. Or a book about my teaching life. But I've given up on that idea. And do you really think I should retire early? It has crossed my mind more than once."

Christopher looked at me. His eyes were still so large and piercing, with lashes that would make any woman jealous, even in death. "Yes, of course I think you should retire. You're not getting any younger, you know. Look at the lines around your eyes. You have more grey hair now, more and more every day."

"No, I do not."

"You do, but the grey hair makes you look distinguished. Looking older brings with it a certain kind of power, you know. People tend to look at you differently when you appear to be older; they're very shallow that way. And you're still beautiful to me. You'll always be beautiful to me."

"You have a sweet mouth."

"Just for you."

"So do you really think I should retire early? I mean, would I have enough money to live on?"

"Look, in this country, it will never be enough. But so what? You never know how long you're going to have to enjoy the rest of your life."

"There *is* so much I want to do..."

"Then what are you waiting for?"

"I still think I have some years of teaching left within me, Christopher. I think I shouldn't waste my remaining years *not* making a difference in the world, don't you agree? I still feel as if I've not been the best teacher that I could possibly be. Didn't you ever feel that way about yourself?"

"There's only so much we can do, Rose. I've said this before, and I'll say it again. I really believe you've done your best as a teacher. Nobody's perfect and we've both made mistakes. And you know what, ultimately, somebody will always replace us. We're nothing in the larger scheme of things. We think our best really matters in the end, but after a while, don't you think we only ever matter in our own heads? We may touch a few people here and there, even change a few lives, but after all is said and done, what was left for us—what did we get out of it? A monthly salary and a few tokens of appreciation. Let's not overrate our profession and ourselves too much, Rose. We did far more than we were supposed to do. Now it's time for the universe to do something for us. Because we die, Rose. We really, truly die. I'm dead now. And you'll die too. But before you do, I want to see you take back something for yourself. You've given so much of yourself. I've seen you give so much, Rose—especially to me. Now it's time to take something back for yourself."

I did not reply. But when I tried to answer, the vision of Christopher began to tremble and soon he was fading, and so did the glowing church around us. The dream was ending, whether I yearned for it to continue or not.

CHAPTER 13

A YEAR HAD passed after Amir's suicide. He was mostly forgotten by everyone except me. Students had come and gone. They easily forgot their previous classmates when they had more exams to study for in the new year, and more friends to make in their newly assigned classrooms, or in their new junior colleges once they graduated. Teachers became busy working on new syllabi. As before, the principal, Mr Ong, was busy shaking parents' hands, the hands of new teachers who had just joined the staff, the hands of those retiring, disciplining and expelling students, chairing and attending countless official meetings, conducting school assemblies, etc. Other than me, nobody in school had known why Amir had done what he did, and neither had they cared enough to find out. The mystery had soon become a non-event, an uninteresting tragedy that became not worth recounting or gossiping about, since no tantalising details had been discovered about why Amir had decided to leap out a window.

"It's as if Amir was, in the end, just another statistic," I was saying to Christopher over dinner at our usual coffee shop. "Just another boy's name in the school register."

"But Rose, you almost forgot him too, remember?" Christopher reminded me, gesturing at a Chinese drinks-stall owner who was carrying our drinks over on a tray, but who had forgotten where we were sitting. "You only started remembering him again because you dreamt of him last night."

Christopher was right. I had dreamt of Amir the night before, but for some reason, I was unable to recollect much of the dream. I had been lucidly dreaming a lot, and increasingly so. Yet I could only vaguely remember details and faces the morning after. Did people dream more as they got older? Were dreams ways of dealing with things that we had forgotten to confront in real life? Maybe I was getting old. Dreams, daydreams, fantasies, nightmares...they were all gathering like a dense fog around the dwindling flame of my tired consciousness.

Now as the drinks arrived at our table, Christopher searched in his pockets for exact change to pass to the stall owner. I was certain that the previous night's dream had centred on Amir and his father. I was convinced the dream had something important to say; there was a moral lesson in it, something that could potentially resolve my guilt about Amir, which I was sure I had been carrying since his death, whether I was fully conscious of harbouring such guilt or not. There were still random occasions when Amir's voice or face would pop up in my mind, especially when I was not very busy in school (which was not often), or when my students' behaviour or lack of responsiveness could prove particularly frustrating.

An image of Amir and his father fishing together flashed across my mind's eye.

Then I realised what I needed to do.

The next day, during the school's recess break in the morning, I made my way to the huge storeroom that was on the second floor above the teachers' staff room. I had to find that creative writing composition Amir had written about his fishing trip with his father. I was certain the composition would help me glean something important about Amir. I opened drawers and drawers of files, rifling through them until I found the file for his class a year ago. If Amir had been absent or on medical leave that day, I would still have kept his composition. But no matter how many times I flipped through the wrinkly pages, with their variations of bad to nearly unreadable handwriting, I could not find Amir's name on any of the pieces of paper. I rifled through the file twice, then thrice and four times, and still nothing. Then I wondered if, by mistake, I had slotted his composition into the file for the class after his. Recess break was almost ending and I did not want to be late for the next lesson. I quickly slid the file back into its proper place in the drawer, and pulled out the next file. This time, Amir's composition jumped out as the first page in the open folder in my hand. So he *had* been absent the day I had meant to return his composition back to him. I strained to read Amir's writing closely now.

Amir's handwriting was almost illegible. I felt the sudden bite of both guilt and sadness. His language was sparse but clear and evocative. I read through his composition a second time. It was very close to what I had remembered: Amir and his father by a lake, his father guiding his son's hand so Amir would cast the line properly into the water, the day bright and sunny as how Amir had chosen to capture the scene. I reread the last line of the composition: *It was a great day for my father and me. I cannot wait for the next time when he takes me out for fishing again. I wonder when that day will be.*

I closed the file, and placed it back in between the other folders in the drawer. Pushing the drawer shut, I wondered if I had just wasted my precious break time doing this. I shut my eyes. In a few minutes, the school bell would ring, signalling that I had to return to class. In the dim storeroom, I leaned my back against the drawers and waited for the bell to sound, still lost in thought. *I cannot wait for the next time*, Amir had written. *I wonder when that day will be.*

While still standing in the storeroom, I started to develop a fantasy that maybe Amir was in a heaven of his own creation, in which an earlier version of his father had joined him. A child on the beach with his father, and his father was happy again, happy to be standing next to his son. Except that Amir, in this heaven of his own design, knew quite clearly that it was all based on a lie. His father was still alive, still existing as flesh and blood in real life, still bitter that his son had been gay, and maybe also remorseful that he had helped to push his son over the edge. Amir was crying because the father beside him was just a figment of his imagination. Amir was crying, but also laughing, both at once; on the one hand, he was glad to stay in the past, as a child loved by his father; on the other hand, he was really in hell, suffering from self-deceit and unresolved issues of guilt over leaving behind his embittered, childless parent on earth.

Or maybe Amir was not in any self-created heaven or hell after all.

Maybe Amir's soul was really trapped at home, watching over his father and his grandmother, watching helplessly as they tried to move on without him, his father waking up later and later every day for work (I realised I had not even bothered to find out what Amir's father did for a living), too melancholic or numb or tired of life anyway to leave the comfort of his bed, his grandmother watching serial dramas on television like she surely did, slowly forgetting she ever had a grandson, forgetting how relatives now looked at them with pity and disdain, hoping she would never have to meet any of them again...

Or even worse, Amir was re-enacting his suicide over and over again. Christopher once told me about what a colleague of his had said about suicides. His colleague belonged to an obscure religion that taught that the souls of those who killed themselves ended up constantly replaying their final traumatic moments for at least a few hundred years. Perhaps that was Amir's predicament now: Amir opening his window, in tears, and angry with his father, angry with his English teacher who had caused all this to happen, angry ultimately with himself for being a useless, gay son; Amir opening his window and leaning out, placing one foot on the ledge, one tentative foot after the other, then stretching out both his arms, then falling; then appearing back in his bedroom again, getting ready to open the window all over again. An eternal loop, perhaps without Amir being even aware that he was caught in a cycle of death.

I shivered.

The school bell was taking forever to ring. I now wanted

very much to leave this claustrophobic room. Standing later in the corridor outside, I wondered if I had time to buy a cup of tea before my next class. I went down the flight of stairs and reached the first floor. A few boys whom I did not recognise were approaching. They stopped chatting when they saw me, and said, "Good morning" in unison as they walked past. I forgot to greet them back, which was slightly remiss of me.

None of the boys had looked like Amir.

The school bell rang.

Later that day, after classes had finished, I sat in the staff room and wrote a letter to Amir's father:

Dear Mr Yusuf,

I'm sure you must remember me. I'm Rose de Souza, Amir's teacher. It's been a year since the passing of your son. I apologise for not speaking or writing to you sooner, and for not conveying to you my deepest condolences before now. I assumed that you would not have wanted to hear from me anyway. Perhaps nothing has changed in that regard. It is possible that you might throw away this letter without even reading it. I hope you do not, because I have something important to say, something that I need you to hear and understand.

First of all, I am sorry if this letter reminds you of things that you would rather forget and put behind you. I know you loved Amir. I know it was my fault for telling you about his problem. It was clearly partly my fault for helping to push Amir over the edge by revealing his embarrassing secret. Even as I am writing this, I am still as sorry as the first time I heard the news about his death.

Did you still love your son when he told you about his secret? Did you say some terrible things to him, things that hurt him enough to make him do what he did?

Are you proud of the things you said to him?

For a long time, I felt guilty and sad that it was my fault that Amir was dead. But I think you should carry some of the blame too.

If you feel like crumpling up this letter now, I would not be surprised; but at least you have read this far, and know that you cannot run away from the truth, which is that Amir also died because of what you said, because of how you rejected him. No son should have to endure being rejected by his own father. I hope you are feeling truly sorry about this, and not burying your head in the sand, not pretending that all of this was due to someone else's wrongdoing.

Amir was not wrong to own up to who he was.

I was wrong to interfere, but I was not wrong in thinking my intentions were mostly correct. I wanted Amir to be happy. I wanted Amir to accept himself and lead a rewarding, honest, authentic life, which is now impossible, due to my interfering ways, but due also to your inability to love and care for your own son.

There are more things that I want to say, but I am not sure what difference it will make to you. There are people who have children for the wrong reasons. There are people who only want children in their own self-image. This is not what parenting is about. Are you one of those people? Was that the kind of father you had become?

Maybe you are feeling sorry after all, in which case, I

apologise for the things that I have written in this letter. I want to believe you might be capable of changing into a better person. I want to believe you might be genuinely sorry for how you behaved. Or you could still be the same man who turned Amir away when he needed you the most.

I don't think I quite care any more. As I am writing this, and in my own selfish way, I am helping to free myself from the past. I want to move on from thinking about Amir and you.

Do you feel like you are free? Do you dream about Amir, and are your dreams happy or sad, or both? What does he say when you dream about him? Does he look older or does he stay the same age? Do you think that maybe Amir has found peace at last? Has he forgiven you for what you did? Would you ever be able to forgive yourself?

I have said enough, I think. If you want to reach me, I have written my home phone number at the bottom of the envelope. If you want to complain to the school principal about this letter, go right ahead. I am not sorry for writing this letter. I am ready for any action that you might plan to take.

Yours sincerely,
Rose

CHAPTER 14

LAST NIGHT, THE night before my last day of school, I had trouble sleeping again.

A memory came to me about my mother. I felt old doing this, haunted by the past at inopportune moments, even as I had in time grown to be accustomed to such mental intrusions. I figured I would one day start babbling to myself like somebody in a retirement home; I might do this even in public, stared at by curious onlookers with no clue that I could be having conversations with the dead. I was fast becoming one of those elderly people who did nothing but dwell on skewed versions of their past. Maybe it was just as well that the next day would be my last day as a teacher; I would not need to inflict my encroaching senility on my boys any more.

In my recollection, Mother was sitting on the edge of my bed in my childhood home. I was maybe nine or ten years old. In a subconscious way, it must have been this memory, coupled with details from Amir's confession, that had given birth to that earlier fantasy of my mother confessing about her sexual experimentations. I was waiting for my mother to leave the room so I (the child-version of me) could sleep and rest for school the next day. Mother had something on her mind, but it was not about lesbianism. She spoke to me as if I were not a child, but an adult (she did not care that I was not mature enough to digest her words): "When the Japanese invaded the country, they blew up my school. After that, they called all of us to gather..."

As she carried on, the whole story unfolded in my head. The Japanese Occupation had lasted almost two years. The entire Eurasian population of the country, including my mother and her parents, had been ordered by Japanese soldiers to assemble one morning on a public field for what they called a 'mass screening'. During this screening, Eurasians suspected of involvement in anti-Japanese activities were forcibly detained. The soldiers pulled away my grandfather, separating him unceremoniously from the rest of his family. My mother and grandmother begged them pitifully to let him go, but they dragged him off anyway. The soldiers let my grandmother and mother go because Grandmother had worked as a secretary in the water department during that time; for some unknown reason, those working in the electrical and water departments were safe from such arrests.

My mother remembered a soldier warning them in halting English to switch their allegiance to the Japanese government and not to take part in any protests or secret activities against the Japanese. Grandmother had insisted that her husband was only a lawyer and had not been involved in any activities. Nobody listened. Nobody knew what happened to Grandfather after that horrific morning; there were only unconfirmed rumours that the Japanese executed everyone they had arrested that day.

I reimagined the scene as my grandmother and mother

sank to their knees in the middle of an open field, holding each other and crying. "Nothing was ever the same for Mum and me," Mother claimed, bowing her head while perched on the foot of my childhood bed. None of them had ever truly been certain that Grandfather had not been involved in anti-Japanese activities. He could have been. Maybe the reason that he had come home late every night was that he had been out plotting with friends about how they could rebel against the invaders, distributing pamphlets or organising potential riots. In my youthful eyes, Grandfather emerged as a kind of resistance hero. Perhaps the Japanese did not even kill my grandfather straight away. Maybe they captured and tortured him; and when he refused to admit to being anti-Japanese, they shipped him off to Thailand to join other prisoners-of-war, where they would be forced to chop down entire forests and cut rocks or build a Death Railway. Their emaciated bodies would finally be buried under the very railway lines they had toiled over, having starved from insufficient food supplies. My grandfather, a tragic hero, a covert defender of his country...

"But he neglected his family," Mother insisted from the edge of my bed. Because of those secret meetings or times when Grandfather did not return home, Mother and Grandmother had worried every day that something might have happened to him. The Japanese had been known for their callousness and cruelty. The Eurasians, being more 'Anglo' than the rest of their countrymen, posed a threat, as the invaders thought it was likely that British sympathisers existed within the Eurasian community. "I was always so happy whenever he returned home, no matter how late in the night, no matter how many times before he came home late, even with Mother shouting at him when he returned, yelling and asking where he had been. My father never yelled at me; he was gentle and happy whenever he was home with us, unlike my mother, who always turned into a different person whenever he was back. She never stopped accusing him of things, of not caring enough about the family, about never being around, about not loving us enough. I knew she loved my father. I knew this because if she didn't, he wouldn't make her angry and sad all the time."

I wondered what I must have been wearing when Mother had spoken to me like this. Perhaps I had on my pink kiddie-pyjamas with the print of teddy bears dancing all over its sleeves. I was not sure who had bought the pyjamas for me; Father could have been the one who bought them during one of his overseas trips; or Mother could have bought it from a nearby market. I tried to recall my childhood bedroom, the row of worn-out soft toys lined up along one shelf, a shelf crowded with books by Enid Blyton and detective fiction written for children my age. There must have been a lamp on my side table, as I had been terrified of the dark. I often slept with the light on, until Mother would creep in while I was asleep to turn it off.

I knew that my mother was saying all this to me because she thought I was too young to understand anything. I was a mindless sounding board for her rants and reminiscences. But she had underestimated her daughter's intelligence and memory skills. She thought, or hoped, that I would forget the entire conversation the next morning. In a way, she had been right. I did forget most of it for a while. It was only years later that this memory flooded back. I understood that Mother had been using me as an empty vessel into which she could pour her grief and frustrations, thinking that none of it would leave a mark on her child. But surely she must have seen the confusion in her daughter's young eyes, the difficulty and psychological twists and turns that must have occurred while I listened to her venting about her family. What kind of mother would use her daughter in this way? A selfish one, I concluded. An immature, emotionally unstable person so caught up in her own woes that she forgot about what mattered in the present: her daughter sitting in bed, nervously absorbing the words of a lonely, troubled mother, wanting most of all to go to sleep.

According to her, after Grandfather was arrested and was never heard from again, Grandmother became a changed woman. Over a short period of time, she turned distant and cold. She became sterner with her daughter and lost her temper more often. "She was always screaming at me whenever I did the slightest thing wrong. Even when I fell down by accident and scratched my knees, she would give me hell. Long after the Japanese left the country, my mother stayed the same. She never allowed me to go back to school. She wanted me to get married and move out as quickly as possible. She just...she just wanted me, her only child, *out* of her life. Maybe it was something in my face that reminded her of Dad, I don't know, but I knew she hated me."

Mother had paused at that instant, her voice trailing off. She had not cried; her grief had merely expressed itself through the dissipation of her voice, like a flame flickering out. I had no real memory of my grandmother. I had only ever seen black-and-white photographs of her in albums that Mother would browse through when she thought she was alone, albums I would peek into whenever she was not home. Grandmother had been a tall woman, even taller than Grandfather, probably as tall as I eventually became; maybe she was the one that I inherited my looming height from. Unlike me, Grandmother had been fairer, although I was not sure if maybe this was because of the way the photographs had been taken back then, their overexposure caused by a combination of sunlight and the flash bulb of that antiquated camera.

I remembered one particular photograph in which my grandparents and their only daughter had been sitting outside on a neighbour's front porch, dressed in their Sunday best, posing for an unknown cameraman. Grandpa and Grandma were smiling, his smile unforced, his eyes wide open and beaming with a kind of overwhelming confidence; she grinned uncomfortably, as if she had been holding the expression for far too long; the child who was to grow up into my mother, seated on a bench before them, was not smiling at all but frowning, eager for the picture-taking to end, her body language contorted with restlessness and discomfort.

Then my mother turned to me in my memory, her face half-hidden by the darkness of the bedroom. "I know my mother cared for me, once, a long time ago. But she had grown to despise me. Growing up with her, I learned to hate her too, and Rose, if I ever lose my temper at you, it's because of your grandmother. Maybe it all started on that day on the field when they took Dad away from us, when they took him away to kill him. Maybe that was the cause of everything. And even though I miss your dead grandmother sometimes, I still hate her. She made me who I am, Rose. So don't blame me if I've nothing nice to say about your father when he is never around. Don't blame me when I keep scolding you. Don't blame me because it's not my fault. I've tried my best to be a good mother. I'm an unhappy woman, Rose. I'm my mother's daughter, after all. Some days, I wish I had never listened to my mother and let her force me into marriage. I wish I had just left home, left the country, stolen my mother's money and bought a ticket and taken a ship or plane to anywhere. I could have had a life, a life that was all my own, without a husband who probably never loved me, and without you, without all these responsibilities I never asked for. I could be travelling right now, you know, I could have a university education, I could have been a sculptor, a journalist, a model, a *somebody* instead of just a wife and mother. Rose, I hope one day you'll forgive me for being a bad mother."

The memory ended. Had my mother really said all that? Or was I making things up as I went along? Surely there was more than some truth in what I was remembering. The older I became, the harder it was to tell the difference between fact and wishful thinking.

This memory about my mother also made me thankful again that I had never had children. I might have turned out to be like my mother towards my kids, in the same way my mother turned (against her will) into my unhappy grandmother. And had my mother been drunk at the time when she was confessing everything to me? I had never known Mother to touch alcohol. I might have been only a child, but I was certain I had not smelt alcohol on her breath. I had always felt sorry for Mother and for her dissatisfaction with life. Even when I tried to impress her with good marks in school or with gifts on birthdays and Mother's Day, she would find it in her to say something disapproving.

Some days, I had even wished, cruelly and more than a little guiltily, that Mother would just *die* as quickly as possible, this woman who had spent every waking moment reminding me of how useless she felt, trapped in a life not of her own making. Even when her daughter had grown up and gotten married, Mother imprisoned herself within the confines of her house like the subdued version of a deranged female occupant of a decrepit mansion in a nineteenth-century Gothic novel, feeling sorry for herself and refusing to admit that maybe she too had played a part in imprisoning herself in her own life, when she could have very easily gone out to meet new people, make new friends, even find a lover, or just board a plane to anywhere.

How often had I thought about my mother alone at home, berating the world for all that it had done to her? And when she died—what a relief it had been. I was too old for feelings of guilt now. It was not as though I had directly caused Mother's death. In fact, all that guilt about wanting her dead, which I had carried since childhood, was fully exorcised now. I no longer felt guilty or sorry for a mother who had cared little about her own happiness. All that was in the past.

Why then couldn't I sleep?

Later, after finally falling into a doze, I woke up in the middle of the night and could not return to sleep; in a few hours the sun would rise on my last day of school. So while lying in bed, I decided to let my mind wander. I fantasised about what a version of Amir's home must have looked like, a living room with rickety furniture and an old, slim Malay man with greying hair sitting in front of a flashing television. Everything in the dream seemed to move a tad slower than normal, and there was no sound, like a silent movie. Even the glow from the television flickered in a sluggish way. Amir's grandmother could not be seen, presumably because she was in the kitchen, cooking or doing housework, all of which was beyond the visual scope of my waking dream.

Then Amir stepped in through the front door. He was in his school uniform and appeared tired from school. He had a backpack on his shoulders, which he then proceeded to lower painstakingly into an empty chair situated next to the television. He mouthed something cursory to his father. Maybe it was something in Malay. Maybe Amir said: "Hello, Dad. Have you eaten yet?"

Then Amir's father looked up ploddingly from where he was sitting, his face inscrutably calm. He said something to Amir. The tone and speed of the scene shifted at that moment. His father's mouth was moving more rigorously and at a faster rate now; he was shouting. Now Amir was shouting too, shouting back nothing that I could hear. Amir looked so angry; his face was contorted and his whole body was vibrating with rage. The old man was trembling too, raising his hand and pointing at Amir and making those gaping, twisted shapes with his mouth.

Then Amir sat on the sofa, burying his face in his hands. It was all happening quickly now. Amir wept, his body heaving furiously. His father was standing above him, still waving his finger, attacking Amir with silent shouts.

Why was I doing this to myself, inside the torture chamber of my own mind? I wanted to stop the vision then, but could not. My fantasy was unrelenting: Amir crying, his father still pointing, his face marred by a sneer.

Then Amir looked up from his hands, his face glistening with tears. First he seemed to peer straight at me; I watched all this with an agonising sense of helplessness, before Amir finally looked up at his towering father. Amir's lips were moving again; they seemed to open and close at a normal speed now, which still seemed incredibly slow in contrast to what had transpired earlier between father and son.

His father was taken aback by this. In fact, he froze.

The whole scene froze. Nobody moved or spoke.

Amir was saying something to bring the moment to a standstill.

His father took a step back, a slow but steady step backwards from Amir, as if he had only now needed some space to observe his son (who was still staring at him) from a distance, and to listen carefully to what Amir was saying.

Amir's lips stopped moving, but he continued to stare fixedly at his father. Both father and son watched each other like this for a long time.

Then Amir's father spoke again, his face gripped by a new stillness. Something he said then made Amir lean lethargically back into the sofa, as though he had been pushed into the cushion by a wave of resignation.

Amir's father sat down beside his son.

The boy was now staring down at the floor.

Next his father did something borne out of my deepest hopes and desires: the old man placed a hand on the shoulder of his son.

Amir closed his eyes, as if stinging from the touch.

But he was not in pain. He was crying.

His father was speaking again, no longer angry. He just looked worn out and acquiescent as he spoke to his son, hand still on his shoulder, grabbing it tightly. Amir was smiling; there was no doubt about this. The boy was smiling and looking right at me now without blinking.

My fantasy was an idealised and amended version of what had taken place in real life. This was what could have taken place if things had gone an entirely different way for Amir and his father. The old man forgave Amir for what the boy had told him. Amir was at peace now. And he was looking at me, mutely acknowledging that all was well in my fantasy.

Then the scene started to dim.

Against my will, I fell asleep for the remaining few hours before the sun woke me up again for my final day as a teacher.

CHAPTER 15

ONE OF THE boys (I think it is Zhang Wei) breaks the silence when it seems that the quiet has lasted for too long. "Teacher? Are you okay?"

I am staring out onto the school field again.

For much of my narration, I must have either been gazing at the far wall on the other side of the classroom, staring at the ceiling where the fan threatens to hypnotise anyone with its spinning blades, or swivelling my head to gaze out at the field.

I turn back upon hearing Zhang Wei's question. "Yes, I'm okay. I'm still alive. And my student died because of me. And yes, it was my fault. It has always been my fault. I used to tell myself that what happened was just a mistake that shouldn't have occurred. But I know now it was more than just a mistake. It happened because I thought I had been a good teacher, a great teacher, someone capable of making a real difference. It was my arrogance that led to me making that awful mistake. Maybe if I had been humbler, or maybe if I hadn't become a teacher at all, who knows, maybe that poor boy would still be alive. I'm not saying I was a terrible teacher. I'm just saying I was not as great a teacher as I thought I was. It was thinking that I was 'great' that led to everything going wrong."

Subra speaks up at this point. I must be tired at this moment because I do not even guard myself against anything rude that he might be planning to say. "But Mrs de Souza, you were only trying to help, right? I mean, your student was obviously too depressed. Maybe...maybe he would have, you know, killed himself anyway, even if you hadn't...if you hadn't called..."

He does not finish his last sentence, perhaps suspecting that he is only potentially hurting my feelings even more by talking further. I am surprised by Subra's concern.

"I know you're being kind, Subra," I reply. "But I think I did push him over the edge. What I should have done was to give him space to just be himself, to be sorry for himself. He had to learn to deal with his own issues, to talk, or not talk, to his father, and to live with his own choices."

The word 'live' from my mouth sounds distasteful and darkly ironic, causing me to stop talking again.

I do not reveal to the boys how Christopher held me as I cried myself to sleep for an entire week. I do not say that, as I gaze upon the boys before me now, I am reminded of Amir's face. In my mind, I envision a paper cup of half-drunk tea on the table at the canteen, fast turning cold; Amir's fingers curling tightly around the cup, then letting go again.

You never have to apologise to me. I had said that to Amir at the canteen. By becoming a better teacher, a more attentive listener to any boy who came to me since then with a confession on his lips, by reminding my students any chance I got that there is nothing wrong with being true to who you are, regardless of what anyone thinks, regardless of what society or religion you have been born into (as long as you do not harm anyone in the process), and by telling this story now, I want to believe my life as a teacher has, in fact, been a long, sustained apology to Amir.

I decide to say something frivolous, after the atmosphere of seriousness that I have created. "Oh my, how am I going to bring all these cards and flowers on my table back home?"

Nobody says anything, but a few smiles break out across the room. Yet a hint of an earlier seriousness still clings stubbornly to the air.

"Teacher," says Eric this time. "I think we never stop making mistakes, no matter how old we are. But at least we learn from them, right? We have to keep learning from our mistakes, or else we hurt more and more people. I'm sure you learnt from your mistakes, right? Anyway, I think—no, I'm sure we *all* think—that you're a really good teacher, Mrs de Souza. You've always been so nice and patient with us, even when we forgot to listen to you, or when we forgot to respect you."

At any other given time, Eric would have been made fun of for saying something like this, and out of a sense of peer pressure, the whole class would have burst into a bout of sniggering. But not today. Nobody is nodding, but I can tell everyone is agreeing with Eric in a tacit way.

Or at least I want to believe that they are in agreement. I look at all of them, moving my eyes from one face to another. Maybe Eric is right. I have been a good teacher; not perfect, but the incident with Amir has made me better, not worse. And have I not always been kind and thoughtful and patient, as Eric is suggesting? I can feel the warmth of pride spreading through me. It is nice to feel like this today of all days, my last day of school. I have only been here to speak the truth—my version of the truth—and to pay attention when somebody had needed me to listen. I *have* been a good teacher, after all.

Eric continues: "I know we give all our teachers cards and flowers and crap on birthdays and Teachers' Day every year, but this time I think we really mean what we are trying to say with the cards and all. I mean, we're never going to see you again after today."

"Thank you, Eric," I reply. "It's enough that you remember the things I've said. And not just remember, but really believe me when I tell you that real life *will* eat you up if you let it, if you allow it to rip out the very thing that makes you who are. If you really want to be true to who you are, you have to fight for it. You have to be humble. You have to be observant and attentive. You have to be strong when other people attack you. You have to be brave. And like Eric said, you have to be willing to learn from mistakes, every time you hurt another person without thinking, especially if that person is somebody you care about."

The hour is now up, so it is time to conclude things. "And thank you. Thank you so much, all of you, for making my last day of school a memorable one. Maybe I'll miss being a teacher in the years to come after my retirement. Maybe I won't. But I'm grateful to have met all of you boys. And I hope you've enjoyed your time with me too. I hope you've learnt some important lessons."

CHAPTER 16

AFTER THE BOYS have left the classroom, I contemplate how I am actually going to bring the cards and flowers with me back home. Perhaps there are plastic bags in one of my drawers that I can use. I pull on the first drawer of my table; it jumps out slightly when I yank the drawer (which has gone stiff from usage over the years) completely open. Inside, I notice a small, blue-green, A5-sized envelope wedged at the back. I thought I had already cleared out the contents of my desk; I must have neglected to see the envelope hiding there amidst the few receipts that I have also forgotten to throw away. I carefully pick up the envelope with my fingers. The envelope must be old as it is browning at the edges. I peel it gently open and draw out the folded piece of yellowish paper from inside. It is a letter.

I unfold the paper, instinctively refraining from reading the contents straight away, written in scruffy handwriting, and scan all the way down to the bottom of the page: *Amir...*

I gasp, and my mouth falls wide open. How has Amir's letter arrived here in my drawer so many years after his death? Or more precisely: how did I never see it all this time? Amir must have buried it all the way underneath the papers that had been inside my drawer, papers that I had never thought to remove for years since his death, until this week when I started clearing out my things. Mr Ong, or any of the other teachers, who might have slipped it into my desk, would have told me if there was a letter from Amir. Amir must have come here himself; it must have been on the Sunday after I'd called his father that he decided to come all the way back to school, creeping into this empty classroom, placing the letter in here before making his plans to—

I wish right now that I am back at home, with Christopher still alive, both of us sitting on the couch as he caresses my back and I prepare to read a letter that I should have read long ago, a letter that will undoubtedly sear into my mind like a heated blade. I hold the paper with slightly trembling fingers, and force myself to read Amir's nearly illegible penmanship:

Dear Mrs de Souza,

I am finding it very hard to write this.

It is also making me very sad.

First I want to say thank you again for listening to me that day at the canteen. It meant a lot to me. You helped me to open up and say things I thought I could never say to another human being. After that, I really thought I had become a braver person.

But you really should not have called my father.

I know you meant it for my own good. But you really should not have done that. It was the worst thing you could have done.

I know I thanked you earlier, but I hate what you did.

I really hate that it was YOU who did it.

Why, Mrs de Souza—what did I ever do to you?

What gives you the right to think you can come into my life and make everything hell for my family and me?

Thanks to you my father doesn't love me any more.

I know this because I can hear it in his voice. I can see it in his eyes now when he talks to me.

He told me I was a piece of shit. He also said you are a piece of shit for helping me believe I can get away with being who I am: with being gay.

Mrs de Souza, I want to get away.

I want to go away forever.

I have no one now. My father doesn't want me to be in the same flat with him any more. I have to pack my bags and move out to a relative's home, if any of them will take me. I know that if they knew the truth, they would want nothing to do with me too.

I don't even have you to trust in any more. I just don't trust you to understand what I am going through. I don't trust you to understand ANYTHING.

I just don't trust you.

So now I know what I have to do.

I really have nothing.

So goodbye, Mrs de Souza.

If you think that any of this is your fault, then yes, most of this IS your fault.

But it is also my fault; my fault for being born this way, for being born into this family, for not making my father happy.

I don't believe in Allah.

I don't believe in you or anybody else now.

But thank you anyway, for thinking you could help.

Maybe you did help, in your own stupid way.

Maybe you helped me get here so that I would finally come to my senses.

Maybe now I can really get away.

Amir

This is the missing piece that was left out of my narrative. Its ending has now changed; and with no more boys before me to hear it now, nobody left to listen to my revised and final lesson. They have all gone for their other classes to convey their goodbyes to the other teachers. Instead I am left alone in this classroom to contemplate the new conclusion to a story I foolishly thought I could put behind me.

In this new ending, I have not been a good teacher at all. I have been lying to myself all this time. This letter is proof; a sign and a traumatic reminder. What a fool I have been, the lies I have told myself to overrate my worth. For all my efforts and preening egotism, what I have achieved is nothing at all! What a lousy person I have been, revealed because of this monumental piece of paper, filled with words Amir must have written only hours before opening his bedroom window to lean out into the cool night air welcoming him with open arms.

No tears fill my eyes. Have I gone cold and heartless too? Should not the memory of Amir garner at least a single teardrop? What kind of person have I turned into after all these years? What kind of teacher have I become?

I sit alone behind my table in the empty classroom for a whole ten minutes, barely moving. I look out the window to see some boys casually sauntering across the field to leave the school compound. Some teachers must have dismissed their students early. I decide that I need to remove the flowers and cards from my table. I want the table to look like a clean slate. I open all the other drawers of my table, until I find one that contains some large, black trash bags left by the school cleaner so that he might easily retrieve them when cleaning the rooms. I open one such voluminous bag and use my arm to sweep all the cards and flowers on my table into it, including the files of notes that I brought with me but never used, and will no longer have any use for after today. Before tying the mouth of the trash bag into a single knot, I hesitate for a second before tossing Amir's letter into the bag as well.

Standing up to walk downstairs, I lug the heavy bag with some difficulty down the wooden stairs and towards the general trash-collection area located just outside on the first floor. Using both hands and with some effort, I lift and then push the bag delicately into one of the large green bins. Then I proceed to the staff room, where I make my round of farewells to all my colleagues, none of whom I will miss after today. The school principal is there too; Mr Ong was replaced several years ago by Susan Heng, a short and slender Peranakan woman in her early forties (principals are getting younger nowadays). I shake her hand politely and she wishes me the best with an earnest grin. Even though I have been given a slew of long-service awards by the school, today nobody has even arranged a formal farewell or birthday party for me; everyone must be too eager to get out of school for the holidays. No one amongst the staff even bought me a cake or a birthday present. In a way, it is a fitting end to my time here.

After saying my cursory goodbyes and accepting each person's well-wishes with an almost condescending nod and smile, I make my way back to my glimmering Mazda in the school's public car park. For a surreal moment, I think that maybe there is already somebody in my car, sitting behind the steering wheel. I hope it is Christopher. When he was alive, I would drop him off at his school every morning, then drive to work on my own. When lessons ended, he would walk over to my school and wait in the car (he had an extra set of keys), so that he could then drive us both back home.

But it is just a trick of the intense glare of the sun. Nobody is in the car. I open my car door and plonk myself behind the wheel with a sigh.

"I miss you," I say out loud, not ashamed that I am talking to myself in the middle of an open-air car park. It is still my birthday today. I can do anything I like. "Happy birthday, Mrs de Souza," I then say in the direction of my rear-view mirror, knowing I will never hear another young boy call me formally by that full name ever again.

In the span of three minutes, I start up the engine, turn on the air conditioning, tune in to a local radio station, and sit there as the car hums around me, the unfamiliar (even slightly unpleasant) music floating into my ears. Then finally I kick off my shoes, press one foot lightly down on the accelerator, and drive out from the school compound, leaving this place forever.

About the Author

Cyril Wong is the Singapore Literature Prize-winning author of poetry collections such as *Unmarked Treasure, Tilting Our Plates to Catch the Light* and *Satori Blues*, as well as a collection of strange short fiction called *Let Me Tell You Something About That Night*. He has served as a mentor under the Creative Arts Programme and the Mentor Access Project, as well as a judge for the Golden Point Awards in Singapore. A past recipient of the National Arts Council's Young Artist Award for Literature, he completed his doctoral degree in English Literature at the National University of Singapore in 2012.